SIRIUS

Ascended Masters Light the Way

Understanding Ancient Wisdom for Spiritual Ascension

Darla Cody

Copyright 2015 by Darla Cody
All rights reserved. No part of this book may be reproduced in any form or by any electronic or mechanical means including information and retrieval systems without prior permission from the author in writing.

Library of Congress Cataloging-in-Publication Data

Cody, Darla, 1950-
Sirius : ascended masters light the way / by Darla Cody. -- 1 Edition.
pages cm
ISBN 9781512287738 and 1512287733
1. Sirius--Religious aspects. 2. Spirituality--Christianity. I. Title.
BL253.C63 2015
299'.93--dc23
2015016467 Manuscript Editors
Brian L. Crissey & Pamela Meyer

Manuscript & Cover Designer: Pamela Meyer
Ascended Master Portraits rights purchased from:
FullMoonMeditations.com
Artists: Peter & Birgitte Fich Christiansen fichart@webspeed.dk
fichart.wix.com/inner-realms
Cover artwork rights purchased from:
superbwallpapers.com
Produced by Granite Publishing L.L.C.
Granite-Planet.net

Printed in the United States of America.

For more information visit:
DarlaCody.com

"Ye shall know the truth,
and the truth shall make you free."

John (8:32)

Poem Given by Ascended Master Djwhal Khul
February 4, 2007

I follow you wherever you lead.
I Am not afraid in word or deed.

My heart is strong to take the load.
I will capture the goal!

It is said — we are dead,
But in your world — we are ahead.

We are ahead of the times.
We are residing in Universal climes.

Do not worry about the foe,
Because God is Almighty, and in control.

We are raising humankind to meet the goal.
For every man's heart to receive the gold
of heaven's eternal Light Divine.

Contents

Foreword **vii**

1. *The Aquarian Age* **1**
2. *Moving Toward Christ Consciousness* **11**
3. *Universal Oneness of Religion* **23**
4. *Coming Evolutionary Changes* **31**
5. *Sirius and Cosmic Evolution* **39**
6. *Solar Hierarchy of Sirius* **53**
7. *Space is Cosmic Consciousness* **57**
8. *Sanat Kumara: The Planetary Logos* **59**
9. *Shamballa — Home of Sanat Kumara* **63**
10. *Departments of the Hierarchy* **67**
11. *Who Are The Masters Of Wisdom?* **73**

Contents

12	Sri Sathya Sai Baba	103
13	St. Germain — Maha Chohan, Lord Of Civilization	111
14	What Is Ascension?	121
15	Purifying Yourself for Ascension	129
16	Regeneration of the Body	137
17	Etheric Body & Chakra System	145
18	Auric Field & Psychic Protection	157
19	Intuition & Mental Telepathy	167
20	Group Activities for Service	173
21	The Law of Light	179
22	Opportunities for The Future	183
23	Spiritual Hierarchies	189
	Bibliography	191

Foreword

At 41 I was happily living the American materialistic dream of more money and more parties. My life was running wide — I held two jobs and never slowed down enough to think, much less to smell, the roses. However, my merry-go-round was about to come to an abrupt and tragic end. One day in August of 1991 I was involved in a very bad car accident that left me severely injured. That day my life started on a different path, which was a true blessing in disguise. It forced me to slow down and really take time to think about my life. I began to see how shallow my reality had been in so many ways.

I was not able to work much, because my physical recovery was slow, taking over a year for me to even begin to feel normal again — or what I had thought of as normal up to that point in my life. Being forced into this quieter lifestyle moved me into a questioning stage in my life.

After several years, it was apparent to others that I had changed as well. Even my husband said that I was like a different person. As I began to recognize the changes, I truly contemplated about what really happened to me in that accident. I can't say the change was easy — I tried resisting it, because I knew my whole life would never be the same again. The lifestyle I had been living was one that most people would think was ideal, so I tried to go on as normally as possible, for as long as possible. I was envied by many people who thought I had it made, but on a deeper level I was becoming more and more unhappy.

After three years of unhappiness, I was involved in another car accident, which was when I realized that I must make my lifestyle more spiritual, and I promised myself that I would really get on a spiritual path. I didn't need to be hit over the head three times.

In 1995 I began to go to group events seeking out more spiritually minded people, and I began meditating. I joined the A.R.E. (Association of Research and Enlightenment) in Virginia Beach, which was formed when the famous psychic Edgar Cayce began doing psychic readings for people. In my earlier years I had read some books about him, and I felt it was once again time to begin reading and studying the kind of material they had available for spiritual seekers.

Late that year I went on an Egyptian tour with the A.R.E., which presented another incredible experience when I recalled a past life there. My dreams were so wonderfully vivid that I had to know more. After we returned in early 1996, I went to the A.R.E. and took their course on hypnotherapy in order to find out more about my past lives.

While I was at A.R.E., I had a past-life session that took me back to my first accident. I remembered dying and leaving my body during the two-hour ambulance ride from New Mexico to a huge trauma center in Amarillo, Texas.

As I left my body, I entered a funnel shaped like a tornado, which I could see was turning very fast, like a wormhole in space. There was no wind inside it because I remember noticing that my hair was not even blowing. I went straight up inside this space, which went on for quite some time. It felt as if I had traveled a long way.

I remember floating on some clouds and seeing someone coming my way — a man in a long white robe with shoulder-length, light, golden-brown hair. As he came closer, I saw him more clearly, and I could see it was Jesus. He had an incredible aura that welcomed me with total love. He had beautiful grey eyes that drew me in deeper and deeper. His eyes were spiraling into infinity without end. All I could do was stare into his eyes.

Then He said, "It's time for you to go back now."

But I didn't ever want to leave Him, so I said, "No, I don't want to go back!"

Then we floated along, until I suddenly stood before three very old men in long robes, with long, grey hair, sitting behind a long table. They were called the Board of Elders. As I stood in front of them, they all stared at me, and when I looked closer at the man seated on the left, he spoke to me. It was Moses from the Bible, who told me that he knew me from a past life. Then I was shown different lives from my past and how I had been tested different times as I worked for the Light. Many past lives were brought before me to give me strength, and determination in this life, and to show me how I had persevered despite many trials and tribulations. Then I was told that it would be good for me to return and continue this path, if that is what I wanted to do. I had to choose whether or not to return to my current Earth life at that time. It would be a few years until I discovered that other people have experienced this same kind of thing.

The next thing I remember was lying in a hospital bed in intensive care. I was on a respirator, barely alive, where I stayed for nearly two weeks.

Later that year I had a reading from a woman who told me that St. Germain — an ascended master of the Great White Brotherhood who is helping to teach humankind — wanted me to contact him. She said that he is one of my guides, and that it was time to start my journey. I found I could talk to him on a higher level of consciousness as I had done in past lives, but I just needed to be told about it to consciously remember it again in this life.

From that time on, St. Germain was with me on a very close level. He told me to go to India to the Himalayas. Until then, I had not studied anything about the ascended masters, although I had heard of

FOREWORD

them. He said I had to be in the Himalayas on a certain day in June 1996, but no more details were given at that time.

At this point, the spiritual side of my life was wonderful, but everything else was falling apart. My marriage was basically over, and my two sons were in high school. My family life as I had known it was gone, and my husband and I drifted further apart until we divorced two years later.

Around this time I went to see Sai Baba, a famous Hindu teacher who resided in southern India. It was another fascinating journey with further past-life memories and awakenings. I was on an incredible spiritual journey, and my life had totally changed for the better.

Since my 1991 accident, I discovered that I had been awakened to higher levels of consciousness, and I was becoming aware of more spiritual masters all the time. I could converse with my teachers, which included a full schedule of instructions and training, and different initiations at intervals along my path of self-discovery. This interaction with the masters became my whole life. This has continued over the years as I have continued to study, travel, and learn.

At the winter solstice of 2006, my guides told me to write a book. I resisted as usual, telling them I can't do that, because I don't know how. For the next six months this inner struggle went on, but I knew I was destined to do it. So in 2007 I made my first attempts at writing. Looking back on it, my attempts seemed so feeble, but since I had put the energy out to start, the information began coming. By the winter solstice of 2007 I realized a year had passed, and I was shocked at how little I had accomplished, so I promised my guides that I would do better in 2008. This is really when it all began to come together, although I didn't know the full picture, as usual. Like many of you, my guides only give me a piece at a time, so I just kept working on the book.

SIRIUS: THE ASCENDED MASTERS LIGHT THE WAY

Around this time my guides introduced me to ancient teachings that had come out in the early 20th century. They were very complex and hard to read, which created problems, because they were not laid out in an easy-to-understand format.

My guides told me that it was time for the ancient teachings to come out, not to be hidden as they had been in earlier days. The lightworkers of today who have been attending workshops and conferences for years are ready for more information that will help them move forward on their path of evolution. These lightworkers will be stepping forward to start using some of the practices they have learned, as well as some new ones that will be needed in the Aquarian Age. It is time to help humanity and be of service in the days ahead, which will help them realize how powerful they really are, and how much they can accomplish. They are the leaders of the Aquarian Age, who will step forward and claim their powers within.

The cosmic energy coming to the Earth now is facilitating a new way of life that will require lightworkers to be brave and to be of service to others, while getting back to basics with pure heart, pure mind, and pure intent.

The information I am writing about in this book has been received through an inspirational-level working with the ascended masters of the Great White Brotherhood who have helped humanity for millions of years. I also work with Archangel Michael who has been of great protection and service. He can be called upon for assistance during these uncertain times we are going through on the Earth.

It is my desire that the information in this book will be used to help lightworkers all over the world understand the role they are to play during the Aquarian Age.

1

THE AQUARIAN AGE

The Aquarian Age has arrived, displaying its glory and splendor in a number of growing trends that bring possibilities beyond our wildest imaginations. This new energy has been coming in since the latter part of the 19th Century and has brought together groups that are steadily and silently growing, while powerfully integrating with each other. This is happening through their desire to be of service to the people of the world, not because of ambition or pride. These people are similar in their beliefs, and have a wide interpretation of truth. They are open to God in all things and have a wide acceptance of all living things, whether it be other people, animals, nature, or Mother Earth.

LIGHT WORKERS

Such groups are also known as "light workers," or seekers of the truth in all areas of life, especially on the spiritual level. They don't have rigid belief systems, and they come from all parts of the world. They are made up of different races, religions and philosophies. However, the one thing they have in common is that they seek to be of service to humanity. This growing trend is sometimes referred to as New Age, and their thinking lies behind the new humanitarian gestures that are now happening all over the world, which does not indicate a new type of government, but rather is a foundational change for the new world, which will emerge from helping others.

There are powerful people in the world who are now busy with methods, techniques, and practices that will raise the entire level of thought in their chosen field, including helping others who are less fortunate. Their desire to help the needy comes without any expectation of repayment. They are motivated by love of God, and they seek to help their fellow humans, which is the true meaning of brotherhood.

Other things these loosely structured groups of people have in common relate to not being restricted to any particular belief system. They do not enforce rules or regulations of any kind, and they are not interested in having any personal authority. Neither are they concerned with the old authoritative ways of doing things, so no discipline is enforced by any of the people in these groups, nor is any particular way of doing things imposed on others. They have no special way of living or working. The members of these groups work with improving their connection to God by helping others; they are not concerned with the details of daily life.

There is one general rule these groups believe should be practiced - each person must respect the others' personal beliefs and not try to impose their particular beliefs on them, or try to get them to agree with their point of view. We all have free will, and no one has the right to impose their beliefs or will on another person.

As we progress further into the Aquarian Age, we will see more of these groups emerge, bringing more divine light to the world by helping others. These groups are steadily growing stronger, due to the strength of the cosmic energy coming in today that helps promote these new ways of doing things. This cosmic energy creates new ideas and expressions of helping others and promotes group ideas and actions that help move humanity toward Christ Consciousness.

These groups have been forming and will continue to grow, blend, and come together as a part of the whole, with each person realizing his/her own personal right as a part of the whole. This will produce the blending of all people and will promote communication among the groups. These groups will represent both sides of an issue, which will in turn create balance.

We can be of service in many different ways, and it is up to you to determine what role you can play in the whole scheme of things. When you find your niche or particular talent, you should do your part to the best of your ability to benefit the whole society. When you do this, you are contributing according to your particular talents, which helps the group progress. As we continue to evolve, people will become more unified in brotherhood all over the world. Different religions are now beginning to understand that a fundamental unity underlies all religions, which will allow the simplification of religion as the small petty differences will begin to become insignificant.

Everywhere in the world people are sharing their lives and experiences with others through the Internet, bringing unification and cooperation to the world. This unprecedented sharing shows people the things we have in common with each other, no matter where we live. This increase in interaction can show how we can get along with each other all over the world. Each country has its own culture, but on the individual level we can see that there are really no basic differences. Each person has feelings, problems, family, love, and things they care about. When we learn to respect each person, we can come together in brotherhood, which will create a foundation of understanding to help us come together in peace and love, while promoting a future of unity and brotherhood for the whole world.

Our nation, the United States, must stop trying to police the whole world. We need to clean our own house first and attend to our affairs by helping the people in our own country. Once we are looking at our own attitude and have good will toward others, our country and people will be moving forward again toward right human relationships. When we show good will toward others, it will spread all over the world, as it did in the past.

The Aquarian Age is promoting the realization of love, unity, tolerance, humility, gentleness, and broad mindedness. When we come together on these higher spiritual levels, we bring more of the Christ Consciousness into our lives on an everyday basis, which helps us overcome negative ways like bigotry, pridefulness, narrow mindedness, judging others, over-indulgence, being opinionated, and seeing ourselves as better than others.

More of the good virtues needed today are courage, courtesy, self-reliance, perseverance, care in details, and strength of character. We should care more about a job well done than about how much money we make. Material things are not the answer when it comes to what means the most in life. Most people know that love is the most important thing in their lives. Love never dies, and the material things of this world decay and fade away.

We are beginning to see some of the old ways of materialism falling down, being destroyed to make way for new and better ways of doing things. Soon we will no longer be a slave to money and materialism. The money system will fail, along with the government, and we will see a true barter system created that will be a fair way of trading between people. One item will be bartered for another of similar value, and this system will grow and become a new way of life.

Small groups of people will form, with each person contributing to the whole, which will be the new way of survival for the people after the old system fails. These groups will live similarly to how Native American tribes and other tribal cultures lived around the world, before the white man disrupted their lifestyles.

People everywhere are ready for the Light; they expect a new cycle and a new revelation. Humanity has greatly advanced over the last century: Their demands and expectations are no longer solely for material things, but instead they seek a spiritual vision, true values, and right human relations. We are seeing more people who are ready to think and act on a global level to help their fellow man.

Since the Harmonic Convergence of 1987, a new Aquarian race has been arriving in astounding numbers. Some of the children being born today exhibit clairaudience, clairvoyance, or even the ability to walk through walls. They can lay a hand on a book and instantly know its contents. They can read the thoughts of others around them. Such abilities will become more commonplace as humans evolve further into the Aquarian Age.

Many people today can communicate with the dead by tuning into other dimensions to bring information of a deceased loved one back to family members. Others can perform psychometry, which is the ability to hold something that belonged to an individual, or touch something that was part of a group, in order to obtain information about that person or group. This ability can be developed with practice.

Another sign of change happening today is where animals are beginning to communicate with their owners, learning to speak simple sentences like "I love you", which has been demonstrated on national television. The animals are evolving quickly to a higher level and are beginning to respond to soul development, which will enable them to evolve into the human kingdom.

Animals were not brought to Earth to feed us, as many people believe. They are evolving in their own right and should be allowed to progress on their path without being slaughtered, ill- treated, or hunted for sport. The brain of an animal is not located in its head. The brain they use to think with is located in their solar plexus. Their bodies are evolving much like human bodies did. Humans are evolving into a lighter, less dense quality, more toward an etheric level. The human beings and the animals of Earth are evolving, but the process is different for each group, because everything is evolving in its own way.

The Earth itself is in a process of evolution. It will only tolerate for a time humankind's destructive actions. The Earth's method of self-defense is to use cataclysmic action to bring about changes that are needed to protect herself. When we do not respect the Earth, and we take for granted all the wonderful things she gives us, we have to pay the price. The Earth is a direct creation of God, and she has many powers at her command. Once the Earth gets to the point of being unable to throw off all the poisons, pollutions, and mistreatment by humans, cataclysmic action will occur. If we don't change our ways and protect

THE AQUARIAN AGE

the Earth, she will be forced to protect herself once again by getting rid of humankind in order to express her pristine purity once again.

The totalitarian systems in the world that imprison the free spirit of the people are on their way out. The new energy of the Aquarian Age supports an increasing desire of people to help their fellowman, and develop new relationships with them. These new energies are supporting and helping to develop a foundation for the work along these lines to be done now and in the future.

Governments will probably fall, followed by a new way of living. There will be a period of transition as old systems fall away, when people will be in chaos and confusion. This chaotic time will last until the new ways are put into place. There could be shortages of food, clothing, and shelter, but in times of hardship, people tend to come together, which we will see happening all over the world. We already see new systems appearing underneath the old, such as the back-to-local-food movement lying beneath the grocery store chains. These new systems will be supported, and uplifted by the new Aquarian energies.

These changes will serve to level the playing field for all people. All races of people will come together in love, peace, sharing, understanding, and brotherly love, and a group consciousness will emerge among all the people of the Earth. We will all move forward together.

During the Aquarian Age we will have a new orientation to life, with a new way of thinking, which will be seen all over the world among the masses of people. Christ Consciousness will spread throughout the world, motivating people to higher spiritual levels and away from materially selfish ways. They will let their hearts be involved to raise their motivations to a higher level of awareness of helping others and being of service. This consciousness of responsibility and service will be seen all over the world, and Christ Consciousness will be pervasive by 2025.

The most important thing we can do to help the human race evolve is to be of service to others, which can be seen developing today in the area of volunteer service and in the new way of "paying it forward."

As we progress deeper into the Aquarian Age, many spiritual opportunities are going to be offered to us. We now can ascend in this life while still in our bodies. Since we are now on the early stage of the Aquarian Age, the door to ascension has been opened wide by the Hierarchy, which consists of a group of ascended masters who have lived, worked, and suffered through a life on Earth in the past. They are called ascended masters because they have mastered the challenges of life on Earth while still in body, as we also do today. The first example of ascension of the body was demonstrated by the Master Jesus, who raised His body into heaven right before the eyes of His disciples. His physical body had been dead for 40 days when He was raised into heaven. Jesus did not have to die, but He let Himself be crucified to show people that they could raise themselves up as He had done, to show by example how we can raise our vibration to a level high enough to ascend into heaven. Other advanced souls before Jesus who raised their vibrations high enough to ascend without going through death included Melchizedek, Buddha, and Krishna.

The Hierarchy, or Ascended Masters of the Great White Brotherhood, as they are also known, is the result of human activity and aspiration. These great teachers have mastered all states of consciousness, while incarnated on Earth as men and women facing challenges, just as do. Their desire now is to assure us that we can reach the same ultimate achievement. We might look upon the members of the Hierarchy as being very different from ourselves, forgetting that they are a community of successfully enlightened men and women who mastered the experiences of life in all its phases, as we can do also. They are more than men and women, because the divine spirit in them registers all stages of consciousness and awareness, which enables them to work with humanity and contact people when needed, and to know how to teach us to move forward through the phases of ascension.

Since we are now in the Aquarian Age, we will have many wonderful opportunities to learn from these teachers as well as from the Christ. We will explore how the Hierarchy came to be on Earth, and how they have guided and helped humankind for millions of years.

Blending East and West

It is time to blend the ancient teachings of the East and the West, in order to bring a balanced perspective to today's world. The earnest student who hungers for this knowledge and is dedicated enough will be offered the opportunity to learn more about ascension through the Christ and the ascended masters who are our elder brothers, for they will show us the way.

Our elder brothers await us with open arms to be of service, if we will just give them a chance to be of assistance. They know we have the power and ability to ascend while still in body, just as they did, to raise ourselves up. They are here to help us at the instruction of the Christ. The energies coming to Earth now during the Aquarian Age will allow humanity to make advances undreamed of before now. We must allow ourselves to come from a place of purity in our heart, mind, and soul to open ourselves up to receive the love of the Christ. In this new cycle, one of the most important things we can do to further our way toward ascension is to be a humanitarian, and help our fellow man.

As we evolve on Earth and come together in love and brotherhood, we are bringing the Christ closer to humanity. He can walk among us once again in order to bring enlightenment to humankind. He is returning and bringing His disciples with Him to help all the peoples of the Earth, not just one denomination or another.

During the Aquarian Age we will see the return of the Christ in a physical body. This will not be the same body He appeared in during the Piscean Age, known to all as Jesus. He will manifest a new body to be used during this time period. He has appeared to humanity down through the ages in different bodies, as it was called for at each particular time.

During the days of Atlantis, Christ walked among the people and talked to them without barriers between Him and the people. The master teachers were present in physical form and they were openly guiding and directing the affairs of humanity, as far as free will allowed. The time has returned for this opportunity to happen again. The teachers will walk openly among us, and the Christ will appear in a physical body, which everyone on Earth will see and interact with.

The cosmic energies now coming to Earth are helping enlighten humankind. These cosmic energies will bring order out of chaos and a new rhythm to replace disorder. This energy is bringing in a new and better world for which all people wait; it will create new ways of thought, new culture and customs, and it will nurture the new life and new states of consciousness, of which advanced humanity will increasingly be aware.

We will be on a much more personal level with Christ. You will draw on your emotions to raise your feelings to such a high vibrational level that you will connect on a much wider level that involves all your senses, emotions, and spiritual levels, allowing God to be felt, heard, and fully experienced on many levels.

The three main lines of energy coming to the Earth now are from Sirius, the Pleiades, and the Great Bear constellation. This energy is promoting different aspects of the Aquarian Age, such as peace, love, unity, brotherhood, evolution and group consciousness.

2

Moving Toward Christ Consciousness

You may be asking, "What do we mean when we speak of the Christ Consciousness?" Consider the transfiguration of Jesus on Mount Carmel with James, John, and Peter, an event spoken of in Luke, Chp 9: 28-29, "He (Jesus) took Peter, John and James, and went up into a mountain to pray. And as he prayed, the fashion of his countenance was altered, and his raiment was white and glistening." This story is an example of the path for us to follow that brings us eventually to Christ Consciousness and the Kingdom of God. Christ has always been the symbol of the potency and glory to which we as human beings can aspire and accomplish.

Jesus achieved Christ Consciousness as He lived His life by example through His words, thoughts, and deeds. He brought the love of God to humanity through His selflessness, love, and service. Jesus was a great soul in whom the Christ Consciousness was merged on all levels of His being. He was fully attuned with perfect awareness with the Christ Consciousness, which overlighted Him at all times. He was perfectly aware of His oneness with God, and He maintained this high state of consciousness.

Christ Consciousness can also be understood as a state of consciousness in which the great soul incarnated on the Earth as Jesus became manifest. From time to time there is a great soul born into which the Christ Spirit pours itself as a physical manifestation, and Jesus was such a one. One of the most important things people can do to further their spiritual path toward the Kingdom of God is to perfect themselves so that Christ Consciousness will manifest within them as a channel of blessings to others. When humans were first created by God,

CHRIST CONSCIOUSNESS

before the fall of man, we were in a state of perfect at-one-ment with God — living within the Christ Consciousness — without the knowledge of sin or evil. Then we fell into denseness.

When we knew Christ Consciousness before the fall, we were in perfect attunement with God at all times in a higher state of consciousness. We are now working toward restoring this state of attunement and consciousness before we can become aware of it being inside us at all times. It is possible for us to reach this state of consciousness again, as shown to us by Jesus. We must raise our consciousness up, as Jesus did, to become overlighted with Christ Consciousness once again.

Throughout time, Great teachers have been sent to Earth when its people demanded strongly enough that they needed help. Once again, the time is right for another great teacher to appear so humankind can evolve to the next level. This is the end of the Piscean Age, when the last great teacher of our time was Jesus Christ, and He lived His life as an example for us to follow. He revealed throughout His life on Earth what wisdom and knowledge could do for each of us. He showed us the full expression of divinity, and then showed His disciples how to carry on the teachings as He had demonstrated.

Jesus faced major trials and tests, which we will call initiations. There were five major points in His life that served as examples for humanity:

1. His birth.
2. His baptism in the Jordan River, after which He was severely tried and tested. After His baptism and until His death, He was overlighted by the Christ spirit, which helped Him face the major tests and trials coming His way.
3. His transfiguration on Mount Carmel, when His raiments were turned to white.
4. His crucifixion on Mount Golgotha.
5. His resurrection and ascension.

Sirius: The Ascended Masters Light the Way

He not only passed all these tests, but He also showed us by example how we could experience ascension, as He had done while still in the body. Jesus Christ understood the law of the prophets that came before Him, and He provided us the next step of truth so we could realize that we, as souls from God, could accomplish the same miracles He did during His life. He showed us by example how we can attain these steps back toward God and move closer to the perfection that we knew before the fall. He demonstrated how we can bridge the essential duality of our nature, and bring about that at-one-ment of the human and the divine, which is the ultimate task of all religions.

There are many similarities between the teachings from the East and the West. We find a parallel between the life of Jesus and other great teachers of the East like Buddha and Krishna. Each experienced tests and trials, which also could be called initiations. Therefore, these religions have similar messages for humanity. Consider that there are many messengers, but only one message.

The Christ is considered the teacher of the West, and the Buddha is considered the teacher of the East. Buddha brought Light to the world, and the Christ brought Love, as demonstrated in the life of Jesus. Both teachers worked for the evolution of all humankind. The message of the Buddha prepared the world for the mission of the Christ. In this way each teacher brought Divine wisdom to us, which builds upon the teachings of the one who came before them. Today we have a giant tapestry blended with all the teachings through time to help us evolve and take the steps needed to raise our consciousness back toward at-one-ment with God.

Moving into the New Era

The Age of Aquarius, signified by the water-carrier, gives all citizens of the world the opportunity to come together in a way that has not happened for 25,000 years, the time it takes to make a complete turn of the wheel, through all the signs of the zodiac, back to the first sign — Aquarius — that starts a new cycle.

Christ Consciousness

As we remain in this new Age of Aquarius for approximately the next 2,500 years, we will receive special cosmic energy that will stimulate our human brains into much greater functioning power, raise our consciousness to a new level, and increase our knowledge, intuition, and thinking processes.

As we move toward Christ Consciousness, most people are working to purify their emotional nature of all of its desires, realizing that they must raise their vibrations up to be in harmony with their soul level. Some people are working on actively preparing for the Christ Consciousness level, which moves them further along the path than most humans. In Eastern teachings, this process is considered the third initiation and is also known as ascension while still in the body (or Transfiguration), as Jesus demonstrated on the mountain, when His raiment was changed to glistening white. Attaining the Christ Consciousness level enables you to control your emotions and mind, to always keep them attuned to the will of God, and to not be controlled by lower desires.

We can also speak of raising our vibrations from our lower chakras to our higher chakras above the diaphragm. We seek to keep our words, thoughts, and deeds on higher levels, not allowing them to be controlled by one's emotional body.

Light workers today hear a lot of talk about people or groups claiming to be initiates of different levels and degrees, but they fail to remember that an initiate makes no claim or speaks about himself. Those who call themselves initiates belie that claim by calling themselves initiates or shamans. A true shaman or initiate never makes such a boast or claims to be special or to be put upon a pedestal. They just live their lives in such a way that everyone around them would know that they were full of wisdom, love and compassion, without ever making such claims. Initiates study with understanding and mental unfoldment, which leads to the true use of words, thoughts, and deeds. An initiate must maintain a balance of head and heart at all times.

Good people who would be considered initiates are to be found in every nation, in every church, and in every group where good will and pure heart are working, and where world service is carried out. There is no special group that would be considered the keepers of the teachings of initiation, nor is it their prerogative to prepare people for this unfoldment. The best of them can only prepare people for that stage in the evolutionary process that is called the beginning, or student, level.

We are not to lay the emphasis upon personal devotion to the masters of the wisdom, or to their own organization leaders, but to the still small voice within, our own soul connection to God. For it is the way of the soul where Christ is to be found while striving to understand through self-unfoldment, self-effacement, and self-discipline.

Another understanding of initiation is as love expressing itself through wisdom. This expression is found in its fullness in the life of Jesus Christ. Initiation is not a process that a person undergoes when they join a certain group, because it has nothing to do with societies, special schools or organizations. Christ gave the instruction on how to accomplish the way through His commandments in Mark, Chp. 12:30-31: "'And thou shalt love thy God with all thy heart, and with all thy soul, and with all thy mind, and with all thy strength'; this is the first commandment. And the second is, 'Thou shalt love thy neighbor as thyself.' There is none other commandment greater than these."

Why this triumph of the Christ Consciousness must always be spoken in terms of religion, of church-going and of orthodox belief, is one of the most incredible triumphs of the forces of evil. To be a citizen of the Kingdom of God does not mean that one must necessarily be a member of any church. The divine Christ in the human heart can be expressed in many departments of human living — in politics, in the arts, in economic expression, in true social living, in science, and in religion. It might be wise to remember the only time it is recorded that Jesus (as an adult) visited the Temple of the Jews, He created a disturbance!

Christ Consciousness

What is the church of Christ? It is made up of the sum total of all those in whom the life of the Christ or the Christ Consciousness is to be found or is in process of finding expression. It is the aggregation of all who love their fellow men, because to love one's fellow men is the divine faculty that makes us full members of Christ's community. It is not the accepting of any historical fact or theological creed that places us in rapport with Christ. The citizens of the Kingdom of God are all those who deliberately seek the Light and attempt (through self-imposed discipline) to stand before the One initiator. This worldwide group (whether in the body or out of it) accepts the teaching that "the sons of men are one,." They know that divine revelation is continuous and ever new, and that the Divine Plan is working itself out on Earth.

Christianity has made eternal happiness dependent upon the acceptance of a theological dogma. You must be a true professing Christian and live your life a certain way or be in fear of going to hell — a hell that grows out of the teachings of the Old Testament, which is full of hate and jealousy. Unfortunately, too many Christian leaders seek to control through fear, and threats to keep people in line with this old obsolete teaching.

The essential truth lies elsewhere.

This situation is not helped by the churches when they do not believe in the Law of Rebirth. The spirit of a person is eternal and immortal — we live again and again. We come and we go, and we are divine. We are finding out today that death is merely stepping through a doorway into another dimension of reality. There are many people now who understand that there are many levels of reality, and there is much to do on the other side. Death in this life is not the end of the soul, for it is immortal. The immortality of the human soul, and the innate ability on the inner spiritual level of the individual to work out salvation under the Law of Rebirth, in response to the Law of Cause and Effect, are universal laws, which cannot be changed or evaded.

Today it is beginning to be understood that God is in all forms, within all kingdoms of Nature, and is expressing innate divinity through human beings. A new concept is entering the minds of people everywhere — that of Christ within us — the hope of glory. This growing, developing belief that Christ "is" in us, as He was in the Master Jesus, will change world affairs and humankind's entire attitude to life.

The life of Jesus Christ showed us a new level of eternal inspiration, hope, encouragement, and example. The love He demonstrated still holds the thinking of the world in thrall, a love that leads unerringly to world service, to complete self-forgetfulness, and to radiant, happy living. The words He spoke were few and simple — all people can understand them — but their significance has largely been lost. Different interpretations of His words led to arguments and discussions by theology, which led to the real meaning of His life being forgotten.

The opportunity for us to move toward Christ Consciousness has never been as promising as it is now. The return of the Christ to Earth is bringing special opportunities for all people to take advantage of at this time. Vast numbers of people will take the first step towards the unfolding of the Christ Consciousness and pass through the first initiation, a passage that often takes place without the person's conscious realization on a physical level. The word initiation comes from two Latin words, "into," and "to go," which means the beginning, or entrance into something. On a broader sense, initiation means an entrance into the spiritual life, the first step upon the path of gaining knowledge, understanding, and wisdom. It could also be referred to as undergoing an expansion of consciousness, which is a normal process of evolutionary development. The passing of each initiation, or step, marks the student's passing into a higher class of learning, and into an increased consciousness of God's plan for the world. Initiation is one's ability to see, hear, comprehend, combine, and organize, the expansion of consciousness into new knowledge.

The second initiation is also called the Baptism Initiation, as bread and water are the symbols of the first two initiations. This is not in any way referring to the baptisms held in the churches involving baptismal pools. John the Baptist gave the baptism of water to Jesus, which testified to the purification of the feelings or emotional nature, which must always be a preliminary step to the purification by fire. Jesus had purified the lower emotions such as hate, greed, doubt, fear, lust, and other negative emotions. He raised His consciousness up to the higher levels of consciousness, which represent positive emotions like love, harmony, peace, patience, and all others of a positive nature. Christ was now able to manifest in Jesus, because Jesus had submitted to the baptism of John. This brought Jesus complete purification from His lower-desire nature, and this was when God Himself proclaimed His Son to be the One in Whom He was "well pleased."

It is the return of the Christ that has made these two initiations possible. The first and second initiations are only now possible to humanity as a whole and are directly administered and supervised by the Christ and the Hierarchy. The third initiation, the Transfiguration, is not yet in use by humanity on a massive scale and is administered by Sanat Kumara, the Planetary Logos[1] in Shamballa. The third initiation is undergone consciously, and with an entirely awakened awareness. The third initiation, or Transfiguration Initiation, is the first major initiation. Jesus was tempted by the devil many times after the Baptism in the River of Jordan. He passed His tests and trials, and proceeded on to the third initiation, which was His transfiguration on Mount Carmel with the three people closest to Him. He had demonstrated self-control, and from that time on, He gained immunity from temptation. As an example, Jesus showed us how to raise ourselves up to blend the physical with the spiritual until we can complete a soul merge and become transfigured into a pure atomic body. Jesus was transfigured into a new

---

1. The Divine Being ensouling our planet.

man by integrating the outer conscious man, and the inner spiritual man, blending the higher and lower selves, the soul and the body, into a unification, which raised all His cells to a higher-vibrational level, which creates a body totally filled with light. His countenance and clothing were changed in the twinkling of an eye.

After the third initiation the student is exposed to monadic energy from higher levels and can communicate by mental telepathy with the ascended masters of the Hierarchy. The Spiritual Triad becomes potent as the conveyor of ideas that are transformed by the initiate into ideals for service of humanity. This is also the stage where pure reason and knowledge of the spiritual will makes the initiate an effective server of the Plan. They can become transmitters of energy, for the purpose of the evolution of humanity, to carry out the will of God on Earth in a constructive way.

The Transfiguration Initiation is also known as the Ascension, or Christ Consciousness, and it is what all humanity is striving for — to lead the soul back toward God. After this third initiation, the initiate has the wisdom that enables him or her to know how to further God's plan, and therefore to work as a light in the world. The person knows consciously what has been accomplished and senses something of what lies ahead. Separateness is finished for the person, who now feels and knows that there is no separateness — for all is one essential unity. The initiate knows that there is no such thing as space, as the truth of all oneness has become known. However, there is still the sense of time to be overcome. All the ordinary rules that have governed the life of a person up until the third initiation — with the petty problems and small reactions to events and people — can no longer influence or determine their conduct. These have all been transcended.

People who are awakening to the world of true reality are being made aware of humanity's essential goodness and divinity through kindness, unselfish acts, and light-hearted attitude in the face of difficulty. It is encouraging to know that we have a divine nature that we can develop and nurture. We can raise ourselves up to higher levels of awareness of all possibilities and to the intuitive perception of truth and illumination that all perfected human beings can accomplish. The kingdom of God is within us, and we have an inner body of light that is present, which can be encouraged to come forth in order to manifest in all ways in our lives.

The time has come for humanity to stop believing what they are told and to move to true knowledge through methods of thought, reflection, experiment, experience and revelation. We can know that we have the ability to do the things Jesus did and can actually achieve these things in our every-day world. After each expansion of consciousness to a more deepened awareness, we return to our every-day life and get tested to discover its reality and truth. We find out where this lies within us to reach our next point of expansion, and we see what new knowledge we need. Our task is to understand and use this knowledge for humanity, and ourselves as well. Jesus died in order to bring to our awareness that the way into the kingdom of God is the way of love and service.

Self-surrender to God is one of the most important things we as human beings can do. When we surrender to God's will, we can bypass our own will, which gets in the way. We must ask God for His will to be done in our lives. As human beings we have free will, and God will not interfere unless we ask Him to override our free will in order that His will be done for our highest and best good. He can see the big picture for our soul, but we are limited in what we can perceive as being the right thing to do. If you wish to attain real knowledge and permeate yourself with wisdom, self-will is lethal. In ordinary life, we know self-will only as prejudice, which always destroys higher insight, creating narrow-mindedness. In fact, we must intensify thinking about self-surrender in order to open ourselves up to the higher levels of consciousness. We must be able to move out of the way, and let God work in our lives. Let go and let God, as they say.

When people do not open themselves up to spirit in an attitude of self-surrender, they limit their own thinking, which only keeps them in their own mind with the same ideas and thoughts in a self-restricting circle. I can understand people wanting some proof — if their minds are closed they are stuck in the same thought patterns, and they will not continue to progress. The soul must be empty and quietly able to wait with expectancy to receive — out of the spaceless, timeless, secret, hidden world — information that can come to us as we open ourselves to spirit.

How do we know if we are receiving the gifts of the spirit? Spirit reveals itself as a feeling of being blessed by a gift from the spiritual world, which could be experienced as receiving a blessing, like an answer to a question, or even as granting a gift, for it is more important to give than receive, and we might be shown a way to bestow a blessing, or to help someone else's wish come true.

In the Bible Jesus tells us that the last shall be first. By this He is telling us to be selfless, and that means we are not to put ourselves first. We are to be of service to others without thinking of ourselves. To be of service to our fellow man is one of the greatest deeds we can accomplish in our lives.

Christ Consciousness can come forward within us when we practice the expectant feeling of wanting to know more about the Christ. As our thoughts center around Him, we attune ourselves to His energy, which raises our consciousness to a higher level that allows Him to come through to us. By reading, studying, and devoting our time toward learning more about the different religions, we can understand the oneness of all things.

There are many ways to enrich, purify, and raise our vibrations to more fully align with the Christ. One of the best is to go within at least once a day, using inward-focused concentration or meditation. It is essential to find a quiet time when you can be alone to give yourself time to go within. Quiet your mind, and give yourself a chance to let your subconscious mind come forward. As we practice, we learn to tune out the noise, chatter, and interruptions of the outer world, giving our soul a chance to be heard.

3
Universal Oneness of Religion

When we think of religion, we consider it as being separate, with different denominations, races of people, and the many ways it is practiced today. On the surface it seems that religion came from many different sources, but the truth of the matter is that religion all began with the One God, although many different ways of manifesting the Divine Love of God have been enacted throughout history. These different expressions of God have been carefully planned for humanity to take baby steps to increase their consciousness to the point of realizing their own divinity as a part of God.

In John 10:27-28, we find "My sheep hear my voice, and I know them, and they follow me; And I give unto them eternal life; and they shall never perish, neither shall any man pluck them out of my hand." That is, people have eternal life. They come back again and again to the Earth to learn soul lessons.

John 10:34 says, "Is it not written in your law that I said, 'Ye are gods.'?" Jesus is telling us that we have the same abilities latent within us to do the things He did, and more. Our souls are eternal, and they do not die; it is only the body that dies, and then the soul reincarnates in another body.

When we die, we step through a doorway into another reality, and we never lose consciousness on a soul level. We go to the other side, and we evaluate our lives relative to the advancements we made on the soul level while we were in physical body. Once this is done, we have a period of instruction before we reincarnate on Earth to try to get it right another time. This process is done as many times as we need to learn the lessons required for our souls to advance on the path back to God. In the

Universal Oneness of Religion

Eastern teachings, this is called the wheel of rebirth. All New Testament references to reincarnation were excised by the Council of Nicaea at the beginning of the Holy Roman Empire, as a control mechanism.

We can raise our consciousness to the ascension level while still in the body, and get off the wheel of rebirth. Jesus showed us by example how to do this process. A major step in this direction happened when He was on Mount Carmel with Peter and John, and His countenance and clothing transfigured into white.

The Many Incarnations of the Christ Spirit

According to Edgar Cayce, the renowned psychic of Virginia Beach, Jesus's soul lived many lives and helped to create the different monotheistic religions we have on the Earth today. According to Cayce, Jesus' first life was 198,000 years ago, as Amilius, in Atlantis, when the Sons of God were on Earth in spirit form, and there was no sexual division. Each such soul was both male and female, as was Amilius. During this period humans entered into physical bodies that were divided into males and females and filled with desires for sensual and sexual gratification.

Jesus was sent by God as Amilius to lead the Earth people who sought to keep balance with God, but also to teach those who had gathered to keep "alive in the minds, the hearts, the soul mind of entities, that there may be seen their closer relationship to the divine influence of Creative Forces." (Edgar Cayce) The ascended masters saved some of the souls in Atlantis, they left the other people who were evil there to perish and they returned to God.

Jesus was then sent to Earth as Adam, who lived for many years on Earth, siring three sons with Eve, according to Genesis.

Jesus then incarnated as Enoch, who, according to the Bible, was very spiritual. After a time, God decided to call Enoch up to the heavens and reveal to him all the mysteries of the universe. Enoch had known them once, when he was with God in the beginning, but he had forgotten them. So Enoch was taken up, and was given all the secrets and wonders of creation, and God placed His seal upon him to designate him as the one who would triumph over evil and be the final judge of all souls.

Enoch was then returned to Earth, and his fame was great. Many nations heard of him and his amazing revelations, and the Egyptians called him Hermes. God was so pleased with what Enoch had accomplished that he was allowed to escape death and was taken up directly at the end of his body's Earth life.

After a time the people returned to wickedness and abandoned the ways of love and service, so God sent Jesus back to Earth again, this time as Melchizedek, who became both a priest of God and king of Jerusalem. His influence was very powerful and caused many souls to remember their higher spiritual calling and return to God. As Melchizedek, Jesus taught Abraham how to start Judaism and the Essenes, part of the Order of Melchizedek. Ironically, years later, when He incarnated as Jesus, He was trained by the Essenes.

Jesus then incarnated as Joseph, born to Rachel and Jacob, as told in Genesis. His half-brothers were jealous and hated him because they felt he was favored by their father, so they tried to kill him, but God had other plans. Joseph was taken to Egypt, where he was faithful and righteous, even though he was far from home. God blessed him, and the Pharaoh put him "over all the land of Egypt," as related in Genesis 41:41.

Next He incarnated as Joshua, who led the children of Israel into the Promised Land after Moses died. Joshua had complete faith in God, but the people lacked faith, delaying their entry into the Promised Land for 40 years. Joshua was in the later years of his life, but as military commander, he drove the enemies from the land that God had promised His people — the same land in which Jesus eventually lived in His triumphant life of love and redemption.

Another of Jesus lives was as Asaph, a man of intense faith who loved God and served as a religious musician for Kings David and Solomon.

Universal Oneness of Religion

Asaph was blessed with the gift of prophecy, which was reflected in his writings, which included some of the Psalms. His influence extended far beyond his lifetime, and a musical or artistic guild, known as the "Sons of Asaph," continued for generations.

Another life of Jesus was as Jeshua, who was instrumental in rebuilding the Temple of Jerusalem after the Hebrews returned from captivity in Babylon. During this lifetime, Jeshua was recognized by a prophet of Israel as the anointed One of God who would one day destroy the devil and his influence, and restore the throne of God to the lost and fallen souls.

Jesus continued to bear the seal of God as he lived other lives, influencing all religions that followed the one true God. One such life was that of Zend, the father of the Persian avatar Zoraster. As Zend, Jesus greatly influenced the beginnings of Zoroastrianism, a religion that quickened humanity's spiritual thinking and helped prepare for the final entry, and the perfect life of the Master Jesus.

Master Jesus has been working with the ascended masters of the Great White Brotherhood to bring all of humanity together in oneness on a universal level to believe in the one God who has helped mankind for millions of years. These Beings of Light reside on the star system of Sirius, and they send teachers to us from time to time to help move humanity along on its evolutionary path according to God's will.

Significantly, Jesus also served as one of Muhammad's spiritual teachers on the inner plane, along with Archangel Gabriel. So Jesus not only started Christianity, but as Abraham's spiritual teacher, He also initiated the Jewish religion, and as Muhammad's guide, He helped birth Islam.

Role Of The Great White Brotherhood Helping Us To Evolve...

Lord Maitreya, head of the Spiritual Hierarchy and the Great White Brotherhood, helped Jesus bring in the Christian teachings. He is also the head of the second department of the Great White Brotherhood, which is known as the Bodhisattva or World Teacher in eastern Buddhist and Hindu teachings. It was a part of his responsibility by God to "overlight" Jesus from the point of His baptism in the Jordon River. Lord Maitreya helped to control the flow of this energy so it would not overwhelm Jesus in His physical body. It was stepped down to allow Jesus by His thoughts, words, and deeds to be a living example in all areas of His life to let Christ Consciousness be seen by people as He lived it in every way. Jesus was guided and helped by Lord Maitreya on higher levels at all times, and Jesus was the channel for this energy of the Christ spirit to be made manifest on the Earth. Jesus was given instructions by mental telepathy from Lord Maitreya who helped Him control this powerful energy. Jesus was protected and carefully monitored by the Great White Brotherhood who were carrying out the will of God for humanity.

Jesus was inspired by and fully co-operated with the Christ energy by becoming the channel for it to flow through Him. The forces, ideas and activities other than His own, but to which He gave His full intuitive assent were all carried forward with full understanding and consciousness of method, process, and results. It was an act of free spiritual co-operation, for the good of humanity in the work of a great spiritual Being or Force.

Around 5,000 years ago the great Hindu spiritual master, Lord Maitreya who is the head of the Spiritual Hierarchy and the Great White Brotherhood, incarnated as Lord Krishna, on whose glorious teachings in the Mahabharata, especially the Bhagavad-Gita, all of Hinduism is based. Furthermore, the scribe for the Bhagavad-Gita was Vyassa, who had incarnated as Gautama Buddha in a past life.

So now we have the intertwining of Judaism, Christianity, the Essenes, Islam, Hinduism, Buddhism, and the Order of Melchizedek, all stemming from the same source. Lord Maitreya, who has been known as the Christ in eastern teachings for thousands of years helped Jesus bring in the Christian teaching, and it is the reason He was called Jesus Christ. Christ, Lord Maitreya has also been working with the Great White

Universal Oneness of Religion

Brotherhood of Ascended Masters to bring all of humanity together in oneness on a universal level to serve the one true God, who has worked with the same enlightened souls lifetime after lifetime to help humankind evolve spiritually. They come to us as teachers who lift us up out of darkness and into the Light. These teachers are sent to us by the Solar Hierarchy based on Sirius. They have helped humanity on Earth for millions of years. They have visited Earth many times throughout time and helped to create the great civilizations of the world. Our evolution on Earth is tied to the star system of Sirius and the Solar Hierarchy.

We also have Djwhal Khul, another ascended master, who was a Tibetan Buddhist, who had incarnated as Confucius, beginning the religion of Confucianism. He was also one of the three wise men of the Christian religion, so we have an interrelationship between Confucianism, Tibetan Buddhism, Christianity, and the Great White Brotherhood.

Taoism was founded by Lao Tse, who, in a later life incarnated as a God-realized Siddha Yoga master in the lineage taught by Babaji. Again, we see the correlation between Taoism and the paths of Hinduism and Yoga.

Ascended Master El Morya incarnated as Abraham, the father of Judaism. He was also one of the three wise men in the Christian story, so once again we see Judaism and Christianity correlated through the Great White Brotherhood.

Count St. Germain, whom we already mentioned was Joseph, also incarnated as the Jewish prophet Samuel, and more recently as Godfrey Ray King, the founder of the I AM Discourses. This again, ties in Christianity, Judaism, and the modern mystical occult teachings of the I AM foundation.

Then there is Archangel Gabriel, who was instrumental in founding Islam through the prophet Muhammad and was also the teacher of Mother Mary and her husband Joseph, an incarnation of St. Germain.

Now we encounter the great Master Kuthumi, who incarnated as Pythagoras, and as St. Francis of Assisi, which interweaves the Pythagorean Mystery School with the Christian dispensation.

As we can see, all these interrelationships and associations have brought about the modern religions of the world today. By weaving this tapestry together we show the incredible beauty of all the diverse forms of religion, and yet the oneness of them all.

4
Coming Evolutionary Changes

Everything in the cosmos works in a cyclic manner. A sub-root-race lasts for approximately 20,000 years, and seven sub-root-races constitute a root race. Seven root races make up one world period, and seven world periods make up one round. We are currently in [world period number x], in its fifth root race, the Aryan root race, which began approximately one million years ago, and there will be two more sub-root-races in this root race, which will overlap and intermingle with the incoming sixth root race. The seventh root race will be the final one for this world period.

There must be three changes in the inclination of the Earth's axis during this world period, according to H.P. Blavatsky's *The Secret Doctrine*. Some of these magnetic pole shifts have already occurred, according to scientists. It is a law, which acts at its appointed time, and not randomly, as science may think.

More fifth-root-race people than ever before in human history will take initiation, which will see the Kingdom of God descend to Earth as a result of so many people ascending the ladder of evolution. The return of the Christ causes a great influx of the love-wisdom energy, which enables people to take the Transfiguration Initiation.

We are beginning to see new characteristics in children being born of the incoming sixth sub-root race. Such children are showing up all over the world with wonderful abilities like intuition and telepathic abilities by using consciousness to bridge the fields of science and medicine so as to raise awareness of the human body and the many different ways it can function. This use of consciousness will serve to move us forward on an evolutionary path that will help us prepare for higher levels of consciousness, laying the foundation for humanity to prepare for the Transfiguration Initiation on a large scale. A growing sense of oneness and unity among humankind is required before this initiation can become a reality for the mass of humanity.

The seventh Ray is brought to Earth by the Planetary Logos, Sanat Kumara of Shamballa. It is a certain type of energy that stimulates changes in our society that will create many new thoughts, ideas, technology, and ways to live. It is also affecting the Earth bringing major changes to the weather patterns, along with certain cosmic energy coming to Earth at this time. Our sun is playing a major role with all its coronal mass ejections (CMEs) and massive bursts of energy to strengthen and fortify this new seventh-Ray energy.

At this time there is a double change taking place, for in addition to the effects of the seventh Ray on the Earth right now, there is also the beginning of the sixth sub-root-race, which brings in intuition and wisdom blending all that is best in the intelligence of the fifth sub-root-race and the emotion of the fourth.

Another great event is the foundation of the sixth root race, which is to take place physically in California 500 to 600 years from now. A community will be established there with the Manu (Ruler) of that race — Master El Morya. Beside him will be his co-worker throughout the ages — the Master Kuthumi — who is to be the Bodhisattva (the world teacher) of the sixth root race. Preparations are already being made for this new root race coming in, although it still lies hundreds of years forward, which is but a brief moment of time.

The mind, emotions, and form of body of the sixth sub-root-race has already begun to appear in America, Australia, New Zealand, and other parts of the world. Within a few hundred years the sixth sub-root-race will distinctly stand out and be admired in its young stages in the new world that is coming, while In the old world the Aryan race will continue to mature into perfection. Perhaps later still, the sixth sub-root-race — radiant and glorious — will shed its blessing upon the parental fifth sub-root-race, so that for the first time an ancestral race shall have a serene and dignified decline. This generosity will serve the incoming new root race in its fight against the powers of darkness, opening up possibilities for people such as earlier races have never known.

When the sixth sub-root-race is fully established, it will show certain characteristics — physical, mental, and spiritual — which are not seen in the average person of the fifth sub-root-race, and these new characteristics must be developed one by one in each of the areas concerned. The process of preparation is a long one and may well extend over several lives. So when we look around and examine people, especially young children coming in, we cannot say with any certainty that one belongs to the new sub-root-race, and another does not.

A more accurate statement would be something like this: Very few can expect to show all the signs yet. They should be well satisfied if they show one or two. Even at its apex, the sub-root-race will not be uniform. It will contain both fair-haired and dark-haired people, both with blue-eyed people and brown-eyed people. The most important things to look for are unselfishness, discernment, common sense, and eager enthusiasm for service, accompanied by active kindliness and large-hearted acceptance. He who ignores his own pleasure and thinks only of how to help others has already gone far on the path.

Some physical attributes to look for are delicate, well-shaped hands and feet, thin fingers, oval nails, and especially thin fingers and thumb when seen edgewise. Three types of heads will be characteristic — the oval face with high forehead, the slightly less oval face with broad forehead, and the skull whose breadth is four-fifths of its length. One who is approaching the sixth sub-root-race shows a distinguishing expression, which will soon be recognizable, if looked for. The texture of their skin is always clear and never coarse.

The heads of those from the sixth sub-root-race tend to be dome-shaped, especially over the frontal region, and the low-set ear is absent. The hair and skin are fine; the eyes are luminous and intelligent, but not

COMING EVOLUTIONARY CHANGES

full; the bridge of the nose develops early; the face is somewhat triangular, but not sharp; and the general physiology is healthy, harmonious and proportionate, not at all the "all-brain and no-body type." The pre-frontal lobe formation will be one of the most noted changes, and the child's first three years of life will be the most important. The next crucial period is puberty, when these children are particularly vulnerable to post-traumatic stress disorder because violence virtually destroys the pre-frontal lobes.

The new children being born are empathic and can easily comprehend principles. They are deeply intuitive, thorough and sensitive, with a quick sense of justice. They show no parrot-like intelligence, but they are eager to help others. They also dislike heavy food and often have little appetite. In many respects they are normal children, but they especially need sympathetic and understanding teachers.

Unfortunately, today children are being medicated needlessly, which is hugely affecting them in life-changing ways. It is known that Ritalin can shrink a child's size and weight, and may cause permanent changes in the brain; Prozac can cause violent and bizarre behavior. A huge problem in the United States is how children are treated for ADD (attention-deficit disorder), ADHD (attention-deficit-hyperactivity disorder), ODD (oppositional-defiance disorder), PDD (pervasive developmental disorder, somewhat like autism), AS (Asperger's syndrome), SID (sensory-integration dysfunction), and ASD (autistic-spectrum disorder). These children have unusually high incidents of depression and suicide, regardless of what drug is being used. There have been too few long-term studies on how these drugs affect children.

When kids watch television, they are being programmed by a steady flow of startle flickers that are designed to keep the brain alert. Advertisers often insist that a certain number of startles appear in each show segment, which is part of their contract with the television producer. Startles ensure that viewers see commercials, which are dense with startles. The neurological impact this has on kids is akin to child abuse, impeding normal brain development, decreasing intelligence, and interfering with the nervous system and emotional response patterning.

These startles cause the child's pituitary gland to release cortisol, which overworks the adrenal glands, making us unable to deal with the prolonged stress of the fight-or-flight response. It can take up to 24 hours for cortisol to clear the bloodstream. Some good books to read are Marie Winn's *The Plug-In Drug*, Keith Buzzell, M.D.'s *The Children of Cyclops: The Influence of Television Viewing on the Developing Human Brain*, and P.M.H. Atwater's *Beyond the Indigo Children*, which is about the new children coming in today, and how we can help them cope with the world in which they will live.

Along with the physical changes occurring in the sixth root race, climate will be changing as well. The Earth will undergo seven periodic whole-scale changes, which go along with the changing of the races. During each round, there must be seven terrestrial destructions, three occasioned by the change in the inclination of the Earth's axis. It is a law that acts at its appointed time, and not at all blindly, as science may think, but in strict accordance and harmony with karmic law. Science confesses its ignorance of the causes of changes in climate and axial direction, and, being unable to account for them, denies the phenomena altogether, rather than admit that karmic law alone can reasonably explain such phenomena.

There four such axial disturbances have already occurred since Viavasvata Manu's Humanity appeared on Earth. The first was when the old continents — save the first one — were sucked in by the oceans, other lands appeared, and huge mountain chains arose where none had stood before. The face of the Earth was completely changed each time; the survival of the fittest nations and races was secured through timely help; and the unfit ones — the failures — were disposed of by being swept off the Earth. Such sorting and shifting does not happen overnight, as one may think, but requires several thousand years before the new house is set in order.

The sub-root-races are subject to the same cleansing process, as are the root races. A person who is trained in mathematics and astronomy should study the patterns and cycles of the past and observe that the rise and fall of peoples and nations is associated with what is known as astronomical cycles, especially with the sidereal year of 25,868 solar years. Such study will show how the rise and fall of nations is intimately connected with the beginning and closing of this sidereal cycle. When these catastrophes have occurred in the past it has been tied to the fall of a root race and a civilization at approximately the same time.

Every sidereal year the tropics recede from the pole 4° in each revolution from the equinoctial points, as the equator rounds through the Zodiacal constellations. Currently the tropics are only 23° from the equator. So it still has 2° to run before the end of the sidereal year, which gives humanity in general, and our civilized races in particular, a reprieve of about 16,000 years. Just since 1997, the structure of the Earth has shifted from being slightly egg-shaped, or elongated at the poles, to being pumpkin-shaped, or more flattened at the poles. It has been speculated that this change has to do with the decrease of the Earth's rotational velocity. When the Earth rotates at its proper velocity, it turns as a unit, but when it turns slower, it causes the Earth to tilt in every direction, causing a great disturbance on the face of the Earth. The waters flow toward the poles, and new lands arise in the middle in the equatorial lands, while those at the poles are subject to destruction by submersion.

During the close of the age of a root race, the moon begins drawing harder, and the tides cause a flattening to occur, which causes changes on the land surfaces. Bulging runs toward the poles, causing new lands to rise and old ones to be sucked in which is in accordance with the cycles and the cycles within cycles. The equinox returns to the apsi (same position in relation to the starting point of the cycle) in 21,128 years due to the influence of another cycle, but the circuit of the ecliptic is completed in 25,868 years.

Ascended master Djwhal Khul says that our present continents have, like Lemuria and Atlantis, have already been submerged several times, and have had the time to reappear again and bear their new groups of humankind and civilization. During the first great geological upheaval at the next cataclysm, in the series of periodic cataclysms that extend from the beginning to the end of every round, our current continents will go down, and new Lemurian and Atlantean continents will come up again. It must be noted that Lemuria, which served as a cradle of the third root race, not only embraced a vast area in the Pacific and Indian Oceans, but extended in the shape of a horseshoe past Madagascar, around South Africa (then a mere fragment in the process of formation), through the Atlantic and up to Norway. The elevated ridge in the Atlantic basin, 9,000 feet in height, which runs from 2,000 to 3,000 miles south from a point near the British Isles, first slopes toward South America, then shifts almost at a right angle to proceed in a south-easterly line toward the African coast, where it runs on south to Tristan Da Cunha. This ridge is a remnant of an Atlantic continent, and, could it be traced further, would establish the reality of a submarine horseshoe junction with a former continent in the Indian Ocean.

The Atlantic portion of Lemuria was the geological basis of what is generally known as Atlantis. Actually, Atlantis must be regarded as a development of the Atlantic prolongation of Lemuria, rather than as an entirely new mass of land up heaved to meet the special requirements of the fourth-root race. Just as with race evolution and the shifting and re-shifting of continental masses, no hard and fast line can be drawn where a new order ends and another begins. Continuity in natural processes is never broken. Thus the fourth root race Atlanteans were developed from a nucleus of Northern Lemurian third-root-race men, centered, roughly speaking, toward a point of land in what is now the mid-Atlantic Ocean. Their continent was formed by the coalescence of many islands and peninsulas that were up heaved in the ordinary course of time and became ultimately the true home of the great race known as the Atlanteans, but Lemuria should no more be confounded with the Continent of Atlantis than Europe with America.

5
Sirius and Cosmic Evolution

The Sirius star system is approximately 10 light years from Earth and is one of the brightest stars in the heavens. This star system has been important throughout the ages to many ancient civilizations. All of the more advanced civilizations of the past have been aware of Sirius after they attained a certain level of evolution. The ancient Egyptians based all their religious beliefs on the helical rising of Sirius each year when the Nile River floods in August. One of the shafts of the Great Pyramid in Egypt points toward Sirius, from where goddess Isis hailed.

The Sirius star system is not generally thought to have any important significance until a person has undergone several expansions of consciousness and reached a certain point in evolution. Humanity has now reached the point in its evolutionary path where it needs to be made aware of how important Sirius is to us. We are ready to learn how Sirius helps us move forward into Christ Consciousness. What this means is that we are moving up from the third dimension, where we are consciously residing now, into the fourth and fifth dimensions.

We completed a full cycle as of 2012, according to the Mayan calendar. They believed that we have now entered the Fifth World, which is very similar to the teachings around Sirius. We are now moving closer to Sirius, which brings more enlightenment to humanity. The ascended masters of the Great White Brotherhood indicate that we are entering the Aquarian Age, which is the beginning of a new cycle that will take us forward into the Golden Age in the future.

The Sirians have been in continuous contact with humans throughout history. The Sirians seek to help humankind move closer to God and are helping all of us find our way back to God through evolution. The Sirians are responsible for the most ancient esoteric teachings that we possess today. These teachings have been given out as humanity became ready for them. It is now time for the general public to become aware of how much Sirius and the Great White Brotherhood have helped humanity.

C.W. Leadbeater speaks extensively about Sirius in *The Masters and the Path*. He indicates that the Great Central Sun is the center of this galaxy, and that it transmits energy to Sirius, where the Great White Lodge of Sirius, and Solar Hierarchy exist. They then transmit these energies to the Great White Brotherhood (Planetary Hierarchy), to be used for the evolution of humanity on the Earth. The Great White Brotherhood works with the people of the Earth, receiving their orders from the Solar Hierarchy on Sirius. The Planetary Hierarchy of Ascended Masters work under the guidance and plans of the Solar Hierarchy on Sirius. They are also known as the Great White Brotherhood. The word white does not represent a color, but rather signifies the brilliant white light that emanates from these celestial beings. This energy is also sent to Sanat Kumara, (Planetary Logos), who is also known as The Ancient of Days. He resides in Shamballa, which is an etheric city above the Earth, near the Gobi Desert. At one time this city was physically located on the Earth, but humanity fell into darkness again, and its energy vibration became too low to keep Shamballa on the physical level.

As we evolve, we become more aware of this energy coming from Sirius. This cosmic energy from Sirius gets stronger as we cycle closer to it, as it moves through its elliptical orbit through the heavens.

Our solar system is traveling through space at a great speed, and its movement takes us into contact with other planets and systems in the heavens. As we travel through space, the Earth revolves through many cycles, and moves through many galaxies, having a positive or negative attraction to them as they emit their energies.

The Great White Lodge is made up of a group of highly evolved beings dedicated to the furthering of the Divine Plan on Earth. They have sent many teachers and avatars to Earth throughout time to help us evolve. They function something like a parent and are represented by the Hierarchy on our planet. The Hierarchy looks to the energies from Sirius, which is so much further advanced than we are that our highest spiritual being appears to them as a mere struggling student.

During the time of Atlantis, ascended master teachers from Sirius were here on Earth and walked among the people of that time. They showed the Atlanteans new inventions and assisted them in crystal technology. At that time the ascended masters showed the people how to do things they were not mentally advanced enough to handle, which led to the people turning away from God's divine plan. The people began to use the new technology for selfish gain, which led to their destruction, which let the Hierarchy know that humans must be led along gradually and be allowed to advance slowly, so their mental level would develop enough to understand fully how using technology for selfish gain, or for the wrong reason, could lead to destruction. Humanity must be ready on all levels to handle the powerful information they are being given.

Today the Hierarchy is working behind the scenes, watching our evolution very carefully to determine when they can again move among us, as they have at different times in the past. Once again it is time for us to make giant strides forward as the Aquarian Age has returned to help enlighten humankind. Now, the Hierarchy is ready for humanity to move forward into the Fifth World, and, with the help of the Hierarchy, we can now open up to new spiritual levels. We must take advantage of this opportunity, for it is tied to the 25,000-year cycle of the Earth and the precession of the equinox.

The Hierarchy was here during the Mayan civilization and assisted their culture in establishing the Mayan calendars of different counting systems to measure time covering thousands of years. These ancient

Sirius and Cosmic Evolution

calendars of the Mayan civilization are some of the most precise ways of measuring time still in use today.

There have been several books written about Sirius that indicate how the Dogon tribe in Western Africa is tied to ancient visitors from outer space. The tribe was given information about the star system of Sirius, which has been handed down through time. This information involved detailed facts about the orbital period and the invisible second star of the Sirius system. The Dogons knew of the existence of Sirius B long before our astronomers could see it with high-powered telescopes. This knowledge was so explicit that there is no way the Dogon tribe could have known about them without some ancient knowledge having been given to them. It is speculated that the Dogons could have been related to the ancient priests of Egypt at one time. Much of the culture of the Dogon tribe is very similar to ancient Egyptian styles, although they may appear to be more primitive.

The Dogons have worshipped Sirius for 5,000 years. They have also been aware of how the planets circle the Sun in elliptical orbits. They believe that approximately 5,000 years ago, amphibious gods, called Nommo, came to Earth in three-legged space ships from Sirius. They have described the DNA pattern made by this elliptical orbit created by the two stars as they rotate around each other. They believe Sirius is the axis of the universe, and from it all matter and all souls are produced in their tribe. Their mythologies also state that Sirius is the source of culture, and both the Dogons and the Sumerians believed Sirius was the determiner of time and the calendar. Ascended Master Djwhal Khul also referred to Sirius as the karmic adjuster, because it was associated with creating the illusion of time and space. There is really no time and space, except in our own minds where we are living our lives on the wheel of rebirth until we can break free of these illusions, and no longer be tied to the cycle of rebirth.

Walter Cruttenden, in *The Lost Star,* gives information to support his theory that our solar system is part of a dual-star system, which causes the precession of the equinoxes to occur about every 25,000 years. Based on ancient civilizations and their worship of Sirius, he believes that Sirius could well be a binary-star system with our solar system. A binary star system is a pair of stars that are gravitationally bound to each other, orbiting around a mutual center of mass. Most stars in the Milky Way Galaxy are in binary or other forms of multi-star systems, which might also account for the ancient Sumerians' clay-tablet references to other Suns.

Many different kinds of avatars and teachers have been sent from Sirius to help humankind. Human avatars who arise from a physical Earth body, like Abraham Lincoln, Plato, Buddha, and Jesus, have a much more restricted impact than celestial avatars, all of whom left indelible marks in the history of the Earth, creating big changes for humanity. The effect of avatars is so great on our evolutionary path that the inflow of divine energy transmitted by them to us forever raises the concepts of human thought to new levels.

The Sirius star system emits huge amounts of electromagnetic energy referred to as cosmic energy, which is helping to change the Earth's evolutionary cycle. Sirius and the Sun both emit huge amounts of electromagnetic energy upon the Earth. Each of us has an electromagnetic field (EMF) around us from birth, which is a natural part of our physical bodies that is known as the auric field. This field has been known by science since early in the 19th century, although it is not commonly taught to the general public.

This electromagnetic energy affects us in many ways, and it is coming to us from the cosmos as well as via microwaves, radio waves, gamma rays, X-rays, and more. These waves are not detectable to human beings without instruments, but they affect our subtle energy field, they can be sensed by those who tune into them.

Sirius is a very advanced star system that is leading us along the evolutionary path back to the Christ, and closer to God. We have long felt separated from God, and we feel that we must look outside ourselves for God. But we must look within ourselves, for we are all a part of God, because God gave each one of us a soul, which gives us eternal life. When we feel separated from God, or feel that we are not good enough, we become susceptible to influences that are not for our highest good. One might say that evil is the tendency to support division and ignore unity, which creates greater problems for humanity to come together in love, peace, and oneness.

Sirius is the star where divine love and wisdom enter this universe, according to Djwhal Khul of the Great White Brotherhood, and this cosmic energy then flows from the Great Central Sun into the Great White Lodge in the Sirius star system. These energies open opportunities for the human race to expand its consciousness toward God. This energy flows through Sanat Kumara (The Ancient of Days), who then divides it into seven basic rays that move the members of the Great White Brotherhood (Hierarchy) to progress forward toward higher levels in a cyclic order. It then passes through all the people who are involved in the Hierarchy on all levels. In other words, the Sirian energy motivates the entire Hierarchy and all involved to move forward toward a higher evolutionary path.

The stars that never set in the sky that are nearest to the celestial North Pole are becoming identified today as having the most influence on the ancient civilizations such as Egypt, Sumeria, and the Mayans, among others. These stars are called circumpolar stars, and the ancient civilizations studied how they moved, how energy was being transmitted from them, and how they influenced the people at that time. It has never been determined that Sirius was a pole star, but it is one of the brightest stars in the heavens, and it is very easily recognized. A line of sight can be drawn from Sirius to the North Star.

**Scientists have found that we are downstream from Sirius in this part of the galaxy. Sirius fits the description of the "God Star" in the heavens, brilliantly blazing, one of the brightest stars visible by the naked eye. Sirius A is brighter than our Sun by about 10 times. The other star is called Sirius B, and it is a small white-dwarf star whose energy is very dense and heavy. It generates huge magnetic fields around it, and it exchanges energy back and forth with Sirius A. It has recently been discovered there is another star in the system called Sirius C, which is also transmitting electromagnetic energy. These stars give off massive amounts of energy that travel to our solar system, especially to the Earth.

Around every 50 years, stars Sirius A and Sirius B come into close contact, and they actually trade places in the heavens. This causes Sirius B to come between Sirius A and the Earth. When this happens, it is so powerful that we can actually feel the magnetic pull on Earth. This happened in 1943, and again in 1993, when the Berlin wall fell and led to the end of communism as a major force in the world. Every 50 years when these two stars coincide with each other, the energy of Earth is it stimulated to break down barriers to freedom of all types.

It is time for us to look again beyond our world to the stars, as the ancients have done before us. We tend to interpret everything in terms of personal interest in our own little world, but we are being influenced by the cosmic energy coming from other stars in the heavens, whether we are aware of it or not. Astrologers have been saying this for quite some time.

The cosmic energy we receive from Sirius affects people, mainly increasing their mind energy, which results in the expansion and understanding of the truth as it really is, and it is lasting in its effects. It is felt primarily in the throat, where sound is created by the body. We must learn to deal with these energies rather than dwell upon our individual experiences that make us feel different from each other and separate from God. It is time to leave the pettiness in our personal lives, and begin to look at the bigger picture of cosmic consciousness, so we can learn to expand and grow in spiritual awareness, universal expansion, and ascension to higher levels of consciousness.

Sirius and Cosmic Evolution

All the work done by the Great White Lodge is controlled from Sirius. The Lodge is a group of highly evolved beings dedicated to furthering the Divine Plan of God's Will on Earth. Whenever humanity demanded help from God down through the ages, there has always been a response given in the form of special divine messengers, and angels. According to Ascended Master Djwhal Khul of the Great White Brotherhood (Planetary Hierarchy), "Those who came as the revealers of the love of God come from that spiritual center to which the Christ gave the name "the kingdom of God." (Matt. 6:33). Here dwell the "spirits of just men made perfect." (Heb. 12:23); here the spiritual [something missing?] of the race are to be found, and here the spiritual executives of God's plan live and work and oversee human and planetary affairs. It is called by many names by many people. It is spoken of as the Spiritual Hierarchy, as the Abode of Light, as the Center where the masters of the wisdom are to be found, as the Great White Lodge. From it came those who act as messengers of the wisdom of God, custodians of the truth as it is in Christ, and those whose task it is to save the world, to impart the next revelation, and to demonstrate divinity."

As the Earth moves closer to the star system of Sirius on its great elliptical orbit, we again have the opportunity to grow in consciousness and awareness. Everything works on a cyclic evolutionary path, which moves our solar system through the heavens.

Job, 38:31 refers to the stars, "Who can withstand the sweet influences of the Pleiades?" The ancients knew all things are tied to the movement of the Earth through the 12 constellations of the zodiac. As we move through these constellations, we stronger influences are emitted to the people on the Earth, which determines how people react to these influences by moving us toward human evolution or retarding our progress, according to where we are located in the heavens at any given time.

The spiritual Hierarchy has been working behind the scenes since the time of Atlantis, and today we have the opportunity to draw closer to the Hierarchy and the Christ. We must not limit ourselves to one idea as to how the Christ will appear to us, or how He will look physically. He is totally unlimited in His approach to humankind, and we must be ready to accept Him when He comes to lead us once again.

A basic Christian belief is for you to be "saved" from sin, and if this doesn't happen, then you cannot go to heaven, so you miss out on eternal bliss. Another perspective is the concept that if you do not expand your awareness and consciousness, then you might be considered a spiritual failure, who must be held back for further development somewhere else during later periods. This is where the idea of reincarnation comes into play, because the soul is eternal, but it is held accountable for the words, thoughts, and deeds of the body in which it incarnates while on Earth. The souls of these persons will be given more chances to advance spiritually in another place and time, and they will continue to reincarnate, and develop somewhere else.

We are in the beginning years of the Aquarian Age, which is stimulating cosmic energies from the cosmos to promote enlightenment for humanity.

The Great White Lodge of Sirius transmits cosmic energies to the Earth from the Great Central Sun, which creates a huge triangle composed of the constellations the Great Bear, and the Pleiades, and the triple-star Sirius system. Djwhal Khul says that these factors, working together as a unit, furnish the essential energies that drive our solar system. These three members could also be thought of as a divine trinity with each one expressing a different aspect: the Great Bear expresses will or purpose, Sirius expresses love-wisdom, and the Pleiades express active intelligence. This triangle is the source of energies pouring upon the people to awaken them to the possibilities of greater expansions of consciousness. It is instrumental in revealing to a person on the path of unity and connectedness with all things within creation. There is much to study and learn about this important cosmic triangle.

Master Djwhal Khul offers another hint when he tells us that our system and the Sirian system orbit together in some way around a cosmic center, which may be in the Pleiades. Our Sun orbits Sirius, and as a unit, the two orbit Alcyone in the Pleiades. The notion that Alcyone functions as some type of universal center or Central Sun is noted in other ancient civilizations. In *The Secret Doctrine* by H.D. Blavatsky, she states that "The Pleiades are the central group of the system of sidereal astronomy." In the book, *Esoteric Astrology* by Alice Bailey, she says "They (the Pleiades) are thus considered (Alcyone in particular) as the central point around which our universe of fixed stars revolves."

We find that Alcyone is the brightest star in the Pleiades, and in the Cherokee culture it was believed that the Pleiades is the center of the universe. The Pleiades were also very important to the Babylonians, who called it Temennu — the Foundation Stone. The Arabs had two names for it: Kimah, "the Immortal Seal or Type," and Kesil. its present name, Alcyone, was derived from the Greek word for Peace.

Alcyone is called the "star of the individual" and sometimes the "star of intelligence" by Djwhal Khul.

There are many myths about the Pleiades, and many of them are along the same lines, including the legend of Zeus and the Seven Sisters and the Kiowa Indian story of The Seven Maidens. The Cherokee Indians have a myth about the Pleiades as the Seven Boys, Anitsutsa, who would rather dance than eat. The Pleiades determines the Cherokee New Year as well as the annual times of planting and harvesting. The Cherokee sometimes referred to the Pleiades as the Four Hundred Boys, indicating the many stars in the whole cluster.

The Great Bear constellation includes Arcturus, a star that has a very advanced civilization and has been referred to as a path out of this galaxy, into intergalactic realms.

As we already discussed, the other star system in this very important triangle is Sirius, of course because it transmits cosmic energy from the Great Central Sun to our solar system.

Once the Sirians have helped us raise our vibrations to certain levels, the initiations given through the ascended masters of the Great White Brotherhood go to a cosmic level, and they become interplanetary. Once we reach this level, we are asked to choose which path we want our training to follow, because we have mastered all the tests and trials the Earth has to offer. The initiate can choose among seven cosmic paths after the fifth initiation. At this stage, we are no longer a physical body; we are pure energy. Most initiates follow the fourth path, which is on a cosmic level and is called the Path to Sirius. Attributes associated with the Path to Sirius are cosmic rapture and rhythmic bliss.

The dark side is very strong right now and very clear about what they want. They have their vision and their priorities clearly held, and also their own hierarchy. They are working in many ways to prevent humans from achieving Christ Consciousness.

Now is the time for the light workers to come together and work as a united group to transmute the negative energy and create a new world of peace, love, and harmony. It is still the case that too many are divided and self-centered, thinking that their opinions are correct. There is a diversity in cultures and opinions, so there is competition, diffusion, and no single focus. We must all come together, and forget our differences to unite against those forces that would keep us from moving into a higher level of Light.

Ether permeates all space and transmits waves of energy in a wide range of frequencies. It is tied to the electromagnetic frequencies such as radio waves, microwaves, X-rays, gamma rays, and human auras. Ether is the element of the Fifth Sun, and it is celestial and lacking in material substance, but very real. We will no longer have polarities of dark and light, but a blending of both to create an uplifted higher frequency for all of humanity. The dark forces don't want this, and they are organized to block it. They sought to unbalance the Earth and its environment in 2012, but we moved forward despite them. However, we still need to work together in unity for peace and balance, and to confront the other

Sirius and Cosmic Evolution

side to preserve life. It is time to get involved. We cannot sit back anymore. It is time for constructive action to really make a difference in the world. You are incarnated on the Earth now for a spiritual purpose. You are needed to pray, to send your positive intentions out into the Light, to visualize the Earth being restored to balance and the people being filled with love, harmony, and peace.

In the ancient Vedic teachings everything is based on an ellipse (elongated circle) that cycles through the heavens, bringing the Earth back around from the ages of darkness toward the Light once again. This movement relates to the Aquarian Age, which is just beginning for the Earth and humanity.

In The Holy Science, Sri Yukteswar, one of the greatest sages and scholars of our time, translated ancient material and gave great detail about the Yuga cycles. He was the teacher of Paramahansa Yogananda, who came to California from India, and established the Self-Realization Fellowship. He studied the ancient Rig Vedic teachings that are some of the oldest known writings in the world and found it written that the Precession of the Equinox lasts approximately 25,000 years. As the Earth moves through different parts of this huge orbit around the Great Central Sun, we are exposed to different energies from the cosmos. The Hindu teachings call these different periods of time Yugas.

The descending Kali Yuga period lasted 1200 years, from 700 B.C. to 500 A.D., when humankind was at its lowest ebb. Then from 500 A.D. To 1700 A.D., humanity has been moving toward the light in the ascending Kali Yuga period. Since then, we have been in the ascending phase of the Dwapara Yuga, also known as the Bronze Age, which will last for 2400 years. We are on an upward spiral of Light when humankind will understand different forms of energy, advanced technology, and interplanetary travel. During this age, we will understand that we are more than flesh and bone. It will be discovered we have an etheric body of energy, including the auric field and we will learn how to work with it. Knowledge of all kinds will be accelerated, transforming everything, and we will understand time and space and the full uses of electricity.

The Treta Yuga (Silver Age) will begin in 4,100 A.D. and will last 3,600 years, during which time we will continue to move forward, as humankind lives more in harmony with subtle forces and the natural rhythms of the Universe. Creation is experienced as a symbiotic relationship between the receptive and nurturing feminine qualities and the masculine qualities of reason and strength. Life in this Treta Yuga is marked by a deep respect and understanding of nature and the universe, as well as the human body, which is all seen as an integral part of the cosmos. People living in that age truly understand the oneness of all things and are adept at perceiving the unity of the cycles of the universe, and their impact on human life.

Some of the characteristics of the Treta Age are mental development, where people realize they are composed mostly of ideas. In this age, humankind extends its knowledge and power over the attributes of universal magnetism, the source of different electricities, and the universal laws. Humanity succeeds in piercing the veil of the illusion of time.

Then we enter the Golden Age, or Satya Yuga, for a period of 4,800 years. It will begin in 7,700 A.D., and last until 12,500 A.D. During this age, the Earth will be a virtual paradise and truth will reign supreme. This is the Age of Enlightenment, in which humanity is completely attuned with Nature and Spirit. During this age the people know they are spiritual beings composed of divine knowledge and wisdom. People have complete mastery over time and space, and comprehend the structure and laws of the universe. There is no duality of pain and suffering, or lower levels of thoughts and desires. Everyone resides in bliss, harmony, peace, and divine love.

Sri Yukteswar pointed out that the Yuga cycle is not only tied to the periodicity of the precession of the equinox, but halfway through the process of the turn of the great wheel around the Great Central Sun, near the year 12,500, the ascending energy switches the direction of its flow. It changes to a descending nature as it moves through the astrological signs of the zodiac for the next 12,500-year period. Different numbers have been used to signify the exact time of the precession of the equinox, as it has been estimated anywhere from the 25,000 year mark to as much as 28,500. Sri Yukteswar indicated that the original count of the Yugas had gotten out of true count due to a mistake that occurred during the descending age.

Cleansing processes tend to occur especially around a root race's 12,500-year mark. At such times we find Atlantis being wiped out by the Great Flood in the time of Noah. The axis of the Earth changed, and the face of the globe was completely changed each time this occurred; complete continents were sucked in by the oceans, other lands appeared, and huge mountain chains arose where none had stood before.

6
Solar Hierarchy of Sirius

Helios is the Solar Logos[1] and his physical body is our Sun. His consciousness encompasses our entire solar system. He is in charge of the ascension process of our solar system. The Solar Logos is comprised of three solar systems representing three departments — The Father, The Son, and Active Intelligence — in much the same way that the Planetary Hierarchy is set up. The first department is the Father — life, will, purpose, and positive energy. It is electric fire, or spirit directly from God. The second part is the Son — consciousness, love, wisdom energy, and solar fire, or soul, and equalized energy. The third part, Active Intelligence, signifies form, body, matter, holiness, negative energy, and fire by friction. These three parts must exist to create life from the atom to the most powerful cosmic being. The universal laws govern all manifestation from the smallest to the largest.

Helios works for Melchior, who is the Galactic Logos[2] in charge of helping the galaxy to ascend (this is not the same Being referred to earlier as one of the three wise men.) The most advanced civilization in our Milky Way Galaxy is the Arcturians, of Arcturus, of the Great Bear constellation, which is why the Earth is now beginning to work so closely with the Arcturians.

The three parts of every form are interrelated, consisting of energy that is in motion and circulates; every planetary body in the solar system forms part of the whole — they are not just isolated planets.

---

1. The Divine Being ensouling our solar system.
2. The Divine Being ensouling our galaxy.

Solar Hierarchy of Sirius

Our solar system and its Solar Logos, Helios, came forth from Sirius, which gave birth to our solar system, and the energies of our solar system periodically return back to Sirius, which is the point in our solar system that acts as the point of re-absorption in its periodic transfer back to Source.

Sirius is responsible for all our planetary life, as well as the emanating source of our Planetary Logos, Sanat Kumara. During this process of re-absorption, all units of life are re-qualified into new life-forms with fresh experience, including karmic adjustments.

The goal for the evolution of human beings is group consciousness, as exemplified by the Planetary Logos, whose goal is God consciousness, as exemplified by the Solar Logos, Helios, whose physical body is our Sun into which the cosmic energy from Sirius flows.

Because our Sun revolves around a central point in the heavens and has a special relationship with the three constellations of the Great Bear, the Pleiades, and Sirius, these three groups of solar bodies are of paramount influence concerning the spiral cyclic activity of our system. Their influence is dominant in connection with solar incarnation, solar evolution, and solar progress.

The Universal Law of Attraction, whether it is working on a human, a planet, or a solar system, will cause extraction to occur from the temporary outer physical self and compel it to return to its source. This pull from the higher source is irresistible to the manifested life, and this Law of Attraction works with purpose and within ordered cycles. It causes the higher self of the living being to seek to return to its solar origin. We came from the stars, and we seek to go back to the star we came from in the galaxy, and that star is Sirius. An irresistible, attractive force pulls us toward Sirius, forming a pathway of energy that draws our consciousness toward the divine energies that bind our system to Sirius, which is our cosmic soul center. Its powerful attraction of cosmic energies works through the Law of Attraction, pulling us along the Pathway of Power, uniting our system to its origin. This Pathway of

Power can provide passage in either direction. Sirius is to us the point of power in our solar system, and the flow of energy would at certain times come toward the Earth, produce manifestation, and then be called back home to its origin, which creates a rhythmic action between the two poles, with the Hierarchy representing our solar system, and Sirius representing the other pole.

This huge cycle can be seen as the in-breath/out-breath of God. For millions of years everything expands and grows, which is the out-breath of God. When this gigantic cycle completes, everything undergoes a periodic return as the in-breath of God, which occurs under the influence of the Second Ray[1], as the Second Aspect brings about the periodic appearing and disappearing of all existences, great and small.

Another type of motion to which our system is subjected is that of progress onward. It is the result of the united activity of the seven solar systems that form the seven centers of the Cosmic Logos[2]. This united activity produces a uniform and steady push toward a point in the heavens unknown as yet to even the Planetary Logos.

We must realize that the bodies of all these huge sentient intelligent cosmic, solar and planetary Logoi (plural of Logos) are constituted of living sentient beings, and the brain can't take it all in. The mind simply cannot comprehend such a staggering concept! Yet it is so, and it all moves forward in perfect divine order.

To a person who has developed the power of inner vision, the vault of Heaven can be seen as a blazing fire of light, and the stars as focal points of flame, which radiate with streams of dynamic energy. Darkness

---

1. The path back to the Source can be walked over seven Rays of the Christ Consciousness that emerge from the white light. The seven color Rays are the natural division of the pure white light emanating from the heart of God as it descends through the prism of manifestation. The seven Rays present seven paths to individual or personal Christhood. Seven masters have mastered identity by walking these paths, defined as the seven archetypes of Christhood. These seven masters are called the Chohans of the Rays, which means lords of the Rays. Chohan is a Sanskrit term for law; hence the Chohan is the action of the law of the Ray.
2. The Divine Being ensouling the Cosmos.

is light to this person, and the secret of the Heavens can be read and expressed in terms of force currents, energy centers, and dynamic fiery systemic peripheries.

The main thing for people to work on now is the first two initiations, which can be received by many people on a mass level today. From the third initiation onward, the ceremony is given by Sanat Kumara — the Planetary Logos. This initiation is not yet for the masses, but once we are ready, we will make our first step toward Sirius and Christ Consciousness. Some refer to this as ascension, and it is felt inwardly. Many people are ready to move into the third initiation, which has been happening for about 20 years on Earth to thousands of people. This process will continue to grow and expand in years to come until it reaches a mass-ascension level. The new sixth root race coming in now must be at its height, and it is just now beginning on Earth.

7
Space is Cosmic Consciousness

Space is a cosmic being, and the entire heavens are made up of the appearance of that being. It is not just one being, but many great cosmic beings so powerful that we human beings have no way of conceiving what they consist of, nor what they do to carry out their particular responsibilities in the cosmos.

In order to gain some idea of how this process might work, we can use the example of how we as individuals with our own lives on Earth, can at the same time be a part of society and a part of our environment. We have our own thoughts and actions, which affect our own family and those you come in contact with in our everyday lives, yet at the same time we are a part of the whole of humanity. When we extend this thought to include not only the Earth, but all of our solar system we begin to understand how we are a part of a greater cosmic being — a being who is expressing itself through a greater life through seven solar systems, of which ours is but one. It is the life and the influence of this vast cosmic being in which we all play our parts as human beings on Earth.

Space is the field in and through which the energies from the many originating cosmic beings play. We are therefore, concerned with the etheric bodies of our planet, our solar system, the seven solar systems, as well as with the vast etheric body of our universe.

Another important energy that affects humanity comes from the Earth itself. The Planetary Logos, Sanat Kumara, is constantly sending and transmitting energy from the Earth that affects all humans living on the Earth's surface.

Space is Cosmic Consciousness

When we talk about the expanding universe, what we really mean is an expanding consciousness, for the energy body of this vast being — Space — is the recipient of many types of informing and penetrating energies. It is also the field of intelligent activity of the vast cosmic beings who live around distant stars, in the constellations, and in the universe, all that encompasses the sum total of these separated living forms. The factor that relates them is consciousness and nothing else. The field of conscious awareness is created through the interplay of all living forms within the etheric body of that great life that we call Space.

Each person is a living being with a consciousness, making each one of us a part of the whole, which makes us receptive to some energies and resistant to others and allows us to transmit the energy through us to others. Each of us puts our own individual stamp on this energy as it passes through us.

It is the magnetic interplay between the many vast centers of energy in Space that is the basis of all astronomical relationships between universes, solar systems, and planets. This consciousness, however, makes the form magnetic, receptive, resistant, or transmitting. This consciousness differs according to the nature of the entity — informing or working through a center — both great or small. The life that pours through all centers and animates the whole of space is the life of a being. It is, therefore, the same life in all forms, limited in time and space by the intention, wish, form and quality of its in-dwelling consciousness. The types of consciousness are many and diverse, yet life remains ever the same and indivisible, for it is the One Life.

8
Sanat Kumara: The Planetary Logos

MASTER SANAT KUMARA

The prophet Daniel referred to Sanat Kumara as The Ancient of Days. Not only did he envision Sanat Kumara, but he also saw the son of manifestation being brought before Him. The Planetary Logos, Sanat

Kumara, came to Earth from Venus about 18,000,000 years ago along with 104 Kumaras, which made a total of 105. These Kumaras are divided into three groups of 35 each, and in themselves embody the three major centers of the Planetary Logos, which consist of the ruling department, the teaching department, and the Maha Chohan's department. They are further divided into seven groups that correspond to the seven Rays. Fifteen of these beings form a center in the body of the Planetary Logos. These groups are the focal points for the force that comes in from the other solar centers of the cosmos. And they also serve as the seven divisions of the Hierarchy.

Sanat Kumara has with Him three Buddhas of Activity, each of whom has a department of which they are in charge and through which they help Sanat Kumara carry out all the duties involved with the evolution of everything on Earth. He is a being of tremendous power, who is playing his role of embodying this entire planet. He knows the Will of God for the Earth, and how it is to be carried out. His areas of power include bequeathing, distributing, and circulating the basic principle of life itself to every form that is held within and on the planet. He is known by many names — the Lord of the World, the One Initiator, the Ancient of Days, or Melchizedek. His consciousness and awareness of all forms, contacts, states of being, and possible energies guarantees the evolution of all the people within or upon the Earth.

The Lord of the World and His Council at Shamballa are the only beings upon our planet who know our divine purpose and how it is to be accomplished on the Earth. A human being's chakra at the base of the spine implements the divine purpose, which can only function properly and be used to carry out the divine will of the soul after the third initiation. The purpose is slowly revealed to the initiate during the final five initiations. After the fourth initiation, people lose their physical bodies and are considered to be ascended masters of the Great White Brotherhood. From then on they function in their etheric body of Light. After the fourth initiation, the initiate begins to glimpse the purpose of the Planetary Logos. Up to this point, the initiate has only seen the plan and has been dedicated to carrying it out. Now the initiate must start to fully express the will of God, and carry it out with increasing use.

There are many students in the world who are achieving the first initiation, and there are many initiates who are becoming ascended masters. The sixth initiation is now the Initiation of Decision, whose entrance rules are difficult and rigid. This initiation presents those on the seven rays with a wide range of choices and a great diversity of choice, so the ascended masters will have nine choices of which path to work toward. There is no need for certain rays to follow certain predetermined paths. They can now move forward under their own inspiration with great freedom. The cosmic mental plane is not barred to them, as it has been in the past.

These changes have been due to the successful response of human beings at this time to the processes of evolution, and to the inflow of Shamballa's will energy, and to the progress of Sanat Kumara. When He makes further progress on His evolutionary path, we reap some of the benefits, because we live, move, and have our being within the consciousness of His vast being.

Because we humans have made progress with our level of intelligence, and we now exist at a higher nature, certain earlier initiations are no longer necessary. We have shown that we can tread not only one or two cosmic paths, but all of them, if we get the right training, which has made incredible progress available to our consciousness at this time, and even greater opportunities have been offered to the ascended masters of the Hierarchy.

Sanat Kumara will continue as our Planetary Logos until the middle of the Fifth Round. Each Round has a total of seven root races, as we have discussed, and we are only beginning the sixth sub-root race at this time, according to Blavatsky's *The Secret Doctrine*. We have approximately 16,000 years to go before the end of the Fifth Round.

The Planetary Logos will take a major initiation in the middle of the Fifth Round, but He is preparing for a minor one at this time.

Sanat Kumara has been in physical incarnation with an etheric body since the middle of the Lemurian root race, and He will remain with us until what is called "the judgment day" in the Fifth Round.

The "judgment day" during the Fifth Round will bring much planetary strife, which will make the current world unrest seem insignificant. When this time comes, Sanat Kumara will have attained the initiation, which is His present goal. An entirely new group of human beings will sweep into incarnation on Earth, and 60% of present humanity will be on the path of initiation at that time. The other 40% of humanity will be transferred to another place to continue their development. There will be cataclysms of a worldwide nature during the next 1,000 years; continents will be shaken; and lands will be raised and submerged, culminating in the profound material disaster that will overtake the world towards the close of the fourth branch race of the sixth sub-root-race, which will usher in the infant sixth root race. The exact dates of these cataclysms are not given, but these changes will lead to a more advanced human race. Earthlings who are not moving forward on their spiritual path will be removed and taken elsewhere at this time to evolve in another part of the cosmos.

Sanat Kumara will encapsulate the entire world with His cosmic consciousness, which must be thought of in terms of circulating and freely moving energies that flow throughout Earth's etheric body, and through our human etheric body, under the essential purpose of Shamballa and direction of the Hierarchy.

9
Shamballa — Home of Sanat Kumara

Shamballa was built by volunteers from Venus who came to the Earth some 18,500,000 years ago. The first center of Shamballa was located in mid-South America, and one of its branches at a much later date was in the ancient Mayan civilization. Both of these civilizations worshipped the sun as the source of life in the hearts of all men and women. A second branch was later established in Asia, of which the Himalayan ascended masters that we deal with today, are its representatives, as are the southern Indian fifth-degree initiates that make up a part of the Himalayan branch of the Great White Brotherhood. Their work has changed from the way it was carried out in ancient times.

The city of Shambhala was built to be like the City of the Kumaras on Venus, which is also called Shamballa, and it is the principal city on Venus. Sanat Kumara and his three assistants, or Kumaras, came to Earth to save it from destruction, and Shamballa was built to accommodate them while they are here doing their work. Shamballa is also the home of the Great White Brotherhood, where the ascended masters have the freedom to come and go as they desire. The work they do for the Earth now directly involves the combined work of the Planetary Logos, Sanat Kumara, and the Hierarchy of the Ascended Masters of the Great White Brotherhood.

Shamballa is also called the City of White, for it was built upon a White Island that was created just for this purpose. At the time it was built, it was surrounded by the Gobi Sea, which has now become a desert, due to the changes in the Earth's land mass over millennia. A beautiful carved marble bridge connected the White Island with the mainland over a sapphire sea.

The main temple has a golden dome that is somewhat elevated, with steps and terraces leading up to it. There is a temple for each of the seven rays with its particular color. The temples are mostly white with domes and spires. They stand along a beautiful wide avenue, lined with trees and bordered with flowers. There are terraces, beautiful flame-fountains and a pool with the blue birds of happiness.

Sanat Kumara, the Lord of the World, resides in the main Temple, which is all white, several hundred feet long, with an arched ceiling. His star is suspended from the ceiling over the altar, which is more than 20 feet high. Marble steps lead up to it in several tiers.

The three-fold flame was established here when Sanat Kumara came. They brought the divine Light with them, for the Earth had no light to speak of in those days. When Sanat Kumara brought this Light from God, it connected all things great and small to it, and it flowed throughout everything both on and inside the Earth. It is the cohesive action for the Earth, and a thread of Light from it connects with the heart of every one of us, an action that has sustained each human through the centuries.

Right after Shamballa was built, one of Sanat Kumara's first actions was to incorporate the Great White Brotherhood in the salvation of the Earth. He works hand in hand with the Himalayan branch of the Great White Brotherhood of Ascended Masters. It was decided that it would best serve humanity to have a headquarters at which the mysteries could be taught, and to have a band of adepts (fifth-degree initiates), and Chohans (sixth-degree initiates), who would function in physical bodies and meet the needs of a rapidly awakening humanity.

Those who work at Shamballa have unified themselves on all levels and are in tune with the universal will of God that Shamballa carries out on Earth. This work is based on inner alignment and intuitive perception. We are becoming more intuitive and aware of energy as we evolve, which will become more common during the next two centuries. The Council Chamber of Sanat Kumara in Shamballa is made up of the ones who can carry out His will because they can see the complete process, and there is nothing that escapes their notice.

These mighty beings at Shamballa are bringing the developing world into line with divine Will, as part of one great divine and spiritual plan. The energy of Shamballa is powerful and dynamic, and if its path is blocked, it burns up anything that would interfere with its progress. The energy of Shamballa now comes to humanity directly, because of the progress we have made during the 20th Century. It will not be stepped down, as it had to be in the past. This direct energy channel allows some of us to contact Shamballa and Sanat Kumara ourselves, instead of going through other departments.

The Hierarchy also works with the Shamballa energy of God's Will, which is carried out by the three heads of departments who, under the guidance of the Christ and the three Directors, implement the Will energy. The powerful Shamballa energies flow down to us through the direction and guidance of the Great White Brotherhood, who have helped humanity for millions of years. These energies flow through everything on Earth and through our bodies. We are not consciously aware of it, but it is constantly flowing, and connects us to everyone and everything. We have heard, "We are all One," and this direct link demonstrates how it is truth on all levels. It all works together to lead us on our evolutionary path back to God.

With this influx of energy, humanity will demonstrate an outpouring of love. This task of pouring out the love principle will fall to those who have taken the third initiation, who are working with the Great White Brotherhood of Ascended Masters to assist in this process. We are beginning a new age, the Fifth World, and this is an important time to accelerate this process in a wonderful way. This work will proceed in a more direct, powerful way for the next several hundred years in order to bring us closer to ascension.

Humanity has shown creative love, of which good will and humanitarian efforts are good examples. This expression of love helps us move forward on our path of evolution, and it allows us to work on a much closer level with the Hierarchy than before. We are being allowed more access to the Hierarchy as a result of the good efforts shown by Humanity so far. When we show progress, it allows us to receive teaching and guidance from our teachers.

10
Departments of the Hierarchy

The Solar Logos lets the cosmic energy flow to the Planetary Logos, Sanat Kumara, who is the focal point and head of the three departments of the Hierarchy, which are the executive offices in which Earth business is handled, and each office depends upon the others, and all work is in close collaboration.

Sanat Kumara's three assistants or Kumaras, help Him distribute the cosmic energy along with His other duties. The Hierarchy receives the cosmic energy from the assistant Kumaras and passes it to their three departments.

1. The Manu, Allah Gobi, heads the first department, which works with evolution of form in all things, whether it is the dense physical form of animal, mineral, flower, human being or planet, or whole nations, races, devas, or other evolutions.

2. Lord Maitreya heads the second department and is the Bodhisattva or World teacher who works with the evolving life within the form, bringing in new religious ideas with the development of new concepts for peoples and whole races.

3. Ascended Master St. Germain, or The Maha Chohan, heads up the third department, which blends the four Rays that deal with mind or intelligence, and, by working with the other departments, controls the evolution of the human mind. This department is very important to humanity right now because it is the Ray that is in focus for the Aquarian Age.

Departments of the Hierarchy

First Department or Ray

The first department, or Manu, is not readily available to humanity. He is assisted by Ascended Master El Morya, who is in line for the job of the Manu for the sixth root race coming up as we are now in the fifth root race. Plans are already being put in place for the sixth root race due to begin in approximately 500 years.

The Manu is responsible for carrying out the will and the purpose of the Planetary Logos. He also works in cooperation with the building angels and is involved with changes in the Earth's crust. He and his co-workers direct the minds of statesmen and politicians all over the planet. The first Ray also serves to bring cleansing and change, and breaks down old conditions to move them forward into more productive, practical means of expression. The first Ray is very intense energy, and those who work in this area are chosen for their adeptness at working with energy.

Master El Morya is not doing any teaching at this time, so he has delegated his students to the Master Djwhal Khul, who serves this function for many of the masters. Ray One is very active now, and soon a young initiate will be training to take over some of his former responsibilities.

One other master who works with the first Ray is the Master Jupiter. Not much is known about him, but he is one of the older masters, and he has been around for a very long time.

Second Department or Ray

The world teacher, or Lord Maitreya — an incarnation of Christ — is head of the second department. Through Lord Maitreya flows the energy of the Planetary Logos, and he is committed to guide the spiritual destinies of all humanity and help them achieve ascension.

The second department of the world teacher is the wisdom aspect of the Planetary Logos, and it is the line of His love in all forms of manifestation. Everything is based on divine love that is being expressed by the Will of God through Sanat Kumara. Love is in all things of the Earth and in the many ways it is manifested, such as love in rule, love abounding, and love in activity. This manifestation is supreme and will eventually absorb all others.

The student must show love in their life, and it may be love working through power, harmony, knowledge, ceremony, or devotion. It may be just pure love and wisdom, blending all the others. Love was the source, love is the goal, and love is the method of attainment.

The main work of the second department is teaching and educating all humanity to understand the oneness of all things with God. Lord Maitreya works closely with the Manu and the Maha Chohan. Working closely with Him is his senior assistant, Master Kuthumi, who is being trained to assume the head position of the second department when Lord Maitreya moves into a higher position, although at this time he is functioning almost as an equal. His new title will be the Chohan or Lord of the second Ray or Department. Master Kuthumi is also involved with the externalization of many of the masters on the Earth right now.

The Master Djwhal Khul has also assumed a much greater responsibility now that he is taking on so many students for Master Kuthumi. He is Master Kuthumi's senior assistant of the second department. The Second Ray is the Ray of the great teachers of the world.

The Third Department or Ray

The Maha Chohan, the Lord of Civilization, heads the third department, which deals with the quality of active intelligence, which usually manifests in the field of knowledge and science. It deals with the student thinking about how, why, and where they come from as they seek to understand how we came to be here. The student wants to find out all about creation and the universal mind, so they can tap into its secrets. This department often includes the people who are artists, musicians, scientists, and others.

Master Djwhal Khul has told me that St. Germain has been promoted to the head of this department, and he is now the Maha

DEPARTMENTS OF THE HIERARCHY

Chohan. This whole department has been realigned, and the work of Master Maha Chohan has greatly increased to include the other four Rays. The Master Serapis Bey has moved up to take on much added responsibility, although he still carries out some of his former work as previous head of the fourth department. He still works extensively with devic, or angelic, evolution.

The Maha Chohan works with the principle of Earth intelligence, and he embodies the intelligence aspect of Divinity. He manipulates the forces of nature and is the principal source of spiritual electrical energy. Like the others, energy flows to him from the Planetary Logos. The Maha Chohan receives directives from the Christ, the Kumaras, and Sanat Kumara.

The department of the Maha Chohan is divided into five sections and has been enlarged to include Rays four, five, six, and seven. The Master Serapis Bey previously headed the fourth Ray and department, but this is now being taken over by the Master Paul, as Serapis Bey has moved to the third department. The fifth Ray or department is headed by the Master Hilarion. The sixth Ray or department is headed by the Master Jesus. The seventh Ray or department is also headed by St. Germain.

It is highly recommended by all three departments that humans use meditation to attract the attention of an ascended master teacher. It is always wise to surround yourself with Light and call on Archangel Michael for protection each time you meditate.

By meditating every day at the same time, you are more likely to contact your guides and angels, because they begin to listen for your call at this same time of day or night. To establish communication through continued diligence shows the teacher you are dedicated and truly interested in communicating with them. As the student continues to meditate, each is given information by the teacher.

Think about the kind of things you enjoy doing and the area of subjects you are interested in. Interests in government, or human evolution would be in the area of the Manu department with Ascended Master El Morya. If you are interested in philosophy or consciousness of any kind, you would seek the department of the Christ with Lord Maitreya. If you desire to know the how, why, and where we come from as we seek to gain knowledge, it would be with the third department with Ascended Master St. Germain.

11
Who Are The Masters Of Wisdom?

As we know, the masters of wisdom are also known as the ascended masters who have lived on Earth and mastered all trials, tests, and tribulations as humankind encounters today. They attained enlightenment because they put God first before anything else in their lives. These men and women persevered with their understanding until it grew into wisdom. The information one learns from the ascended masters is learned in steps, usually carried out over a period of many years. The wisdom I speak of here is not something that can be attained immediately. It takes time to learn and digest what has been given earlier, before the next step is given, which forms a base of wisdom the students can use to expand their consciousness into higher levels, where more growth can occur.

The Hierarchy is made up of ascended masters who have learned the same lessons that humans are currently learning. The masters are called ascended masters, because they passed all their tests, and passed on to their ascension. They were devoted throughout many lives to the Fatherhood of God and the Brotherhood of Man. Their service to this ideal gained them entrance into this wonderful group of ascended masters, who have the highest and purest intentions, and who are still working to free humankind from all illusion and suffering, and to help others to ascend while still in body, as they have done in their lives. They show us that it is possible to reach this level of immortality and be free of the wheel of rebirth.

The ascended masters have such a high vibration that they cannot be seen with the physical eyes, unless they choose to let you see them. They can create a body and make it look like anything they want, male or female. Their bodies are not the gross physical bodies like we have, but are etheric and made up of pure light, which has been cleansed of all things that would be of a negative level. We have seen pictures of beings that are pure light — so bright that we cannot look upon them — which is how the ascended masters look in their pure state of being. Angels also have this pure divine white light around themselves.

The ascended masters do not have to eat food as humans do, but sometimes they do, just to give the students the feeling of equality. When they take in food, it is instantly transmuted into light as it touches their throats. They have no digestive organs, but they do have a heart and bloodstream, which is light and golden in color. The heart is the center of the body, and not to the left side as it is in human beings. The divine Light has taken the place of the bloodstream in the ascended masters' bodies.

When an ascended master appears to someone not knowing the law, He/She is permitted by the great Law to hold back the greater part of His/Her radiance, thereby only radiating out enough energy to produce the results required, but no more than the human can withstand. Unless the human has purified himself/herself and gained sufficient self-control, it would not be merciful or kind to radiate the full measure of energy, because when a master appears, His/Her tremendous energy intensifies everything He/She contacts. If there are still undesirable qualities in the individual, those, too, would be intensified. Therefore it might give him/her too much to handle. But, when an ascended master appears to someone who knows the law, however, He/She is not permitted to withhold His/Her radiance.

All human beings have the opportunity to become an ascended being, just like the ascended masters and the angels. During the Aquarian Age, the opportunity to become ascended has been heightened because the Piscean Cycle has ended and we are now in the Aquarian cycle for approximately the next 2,300 years. Many wonderful changes are coming to the human race in this new cycle.

There is a group of these master teachers who are returning to Earth in dense physical bodies to help humanity step into the light, as they have done themselves. They are not going to do this work for us, but they are giving us every opportunity now to raise our consciousness. We can choose to take advantage of this offer or decline it, for we have free will. They do not take advantage of our free will. We must always make the choices for ourselves.

The animal kingdom is also evolving, and it is being made ready to advance into the human kingdom. Animals are learning how to speak and to communicate with people in different ways, especially the pets that people have today, such as dogs, cats, and birds.

Another indication of time speeding up is the new development we see in the field of communications, such as the Internet, sending and receiving information instantly, showing us how quickly we can interact with others in any part of the world. Worldwide communications are working to bring people together on a universal level.

The door to ascension has been opened wide by the Hierarchy, and as we progress deeper into the Aquarian Age, many spiritual opportunities are going to be offered to us. We will find out how to ascend while still in our bodies. The first example of ascension that has been shown to us is the Master Jesus, who raised His body into heaven right before the eyes of His disciples. His physical body had been dead for 40 days when He was raised into heaven. Jesus did not have to die, but He let Himself be crucified to show people how they could raise themselves up as He had done. He showed us by example how we humans can raise our vibrations high enough to ascend into heaven. There were humans who were raising their vibrations to ascension level without going through death long before Jesus, and among them were Melchizedek and Krishna, Buddha, and other advanced souls. We will explore how the Hierarchy came to be here on Earth, and how they have guided and helped humankind for millions of years.

Who Are The Masters Of Wisdom?

It is important for us to remember that the ascended masters mastered all states of consciousness as men and women facing challenges while they were living lives on Earth, just as we do every day, which assures us that we can reach the same ultimate achievement. We might look upon the members of the Hierarchy as being very different from ourselves, forgetting that the Hierarchy is a community of spiritually successful men and women. Their own experiences enable them to work with humanity, to contact people when needed, and to know how to teach us to move forward through the phases of ascension.

It is time to blend the ancient teachings of the East and the West, in order to bring a balanced perspective to the world. The earnest students who hunger for this knowledge and are dedicated enough to put it first in their lives will be offered the opportunity to ascend through Christ and the ascended masters, who are ready to show us the way.

Our elder brothers await us with open arms, ready to be of service, if we will just give them a chance to help. They know that we have the power and ability to ascend while still in the body, as they have done before us. They are here to help us, at the instruction of the Christ.

As we evolve on Earth, we will be coming together in love and brotherhood and bringing Christ closer to humanity. He can walk among us once again in order to bring enlightenment to all of humankind. He is returning and bringing his disciples with Him to help all the people of the Earth, not just one denomination or another.

During the days of Atlantis, Christ walked among the people, He talked to them, and there were no barriers between Him and the people. The master teachers were present in physical form, and they were openly guiding and directing the affairs of humanity, as far as free will allowed. The time has returned for this to happen again. The teachers will walk openly among us, and the Christ will appear in a physical body that everyone can see and interact with.

The cosmic energies now coming to the Earth are helping enlighten humanity. They will bring order out of chaos and rhythm to replace disorder. This energy is bringing in a new and better world for which all people wait; it will create new ways of thought, new culture, and customs, and it will nurture the new life and new states of consciousness, of which advanced humanity will increasingly be aware.

There are six masters of the Hierarchy who are preparing the way for the Christ to return to walk openly among the people once again. They are Master El Morya, Master Djwhal Khul, Master Kuthumi, Master St. Germain, Master Hilarion, and Master Paul. These consecrated workers form a nucleus around the Christ, and direct much of the preparatory work.

The Buddha

Siddhartha Gautama was born around 563 B.C. He was in line to become the emperor, however, his compassion for the suffering of others directed him onto the spiritual path. He had led a pampered life until he saw all the pain and suffering in the world. From that moment on, he renounced his position as the emperor's son, and chose an ascetic life. Those experiences molded his philosophy of following the Middle Way, a life of moderation rather than extremes. He was the first human to attain the necessary enlightenment that qualified him for the position of "Buddha" in the Planetary Hierarchy. He anchored the Lighted Way, its revelations, and its effects in consciousness 2500 years ago. Then Jesus and Lord Maitreya came 500 years later to anchor the full expression of Love/Wisdom. The Christ completed Buddha's work, permitting the full expression of Love/Wisdom in its dual aspect to become one.

Lord Gautama, The Buddha, has a special type of force and blessing outpoured once each year at the time of the Wesak Festival, which is held at the third full moon after the spring equinox. This usually takes place in May. This is celebrated each year to honor the date of his ascension, which happened at the time of the full moon of May in 544 B.C. He was transformed into the fully enlightened Buddha. The Wesak Festival is the celebration held in honor of the wonderful occurrences in the last life of the Buddha, including His birth, His attainment of

THE BUDDHA

Buddhahood, and His departure from the physical body. The Wesak Festival is honored by an appearance of the Buddha each year over the Himalayas. He appears to float above the mountains of the Himalayas, and he looks enormous. He is sitting cross-legged with hands together, as

He floats in the heavens, dressed in the yellow robe of the Buddhist monk, but wearing it so as to leave His right arm bare.

His face is truly Godlike, combining calmness, power, wisdom, and love, in an expression of the Divine. His complexion is yellowish-white, His features are clear-cut, and His forehead is broad and noble, His eyes are large, luminous, and deep, dark blue. He has a slightly aquiline nose, with firmly set red lips. He wears his black hair just above the shoulders parted in the center, and swept back from His forehead.

A splendid aura emanates from Him in rings of iridescent colors, interspersed with flashes of green and violet. He is enclosed in Light so bright that it is hard to gaze upon, but His face and color of His robe stand out.

The Buddha can access planes of consciousness that are altogether beyond our reach, which allows Him to transmute, and draw down special blessings to humanity. Without the Buddha bringing these high vibrations to us, they would be beyond our reach, and we would not receive their benefits. Since He has consented to do this blessing for humanity, all people benefit from it all over the world. It strengthens all good work, and brings peace to the hearts of those who can receive it.

Lord Maitreya and Krishna

The Christ Spirit incarnated as both Lord Maitreya and the great Hindu Master Krishna, one of the greatest Eastern masters the world has known. He also occupied occasionally the body of Tsong-ka-pa, the great Tibetan religious reformer. He sent forth a stream of pupils throughout the centuries, including Nagarjuna, Aryasanga, Ramanujacharya, Madhavacharya, and many others, who founded new sects or threw new light upon the mysteries of religion. He also sent out a pupil to found Islam. Sending out teachers was only a part of his work, which is not confined to humanity, but which also includes the education of all Earth creatures and the Devic evolution of the angel kingdom. He is the head of all current faiths.

KRISHNA

During this time period, He will gather around all the souls who have helped establish new civilizations in the past. He will bring this group together once again around the time of his last life, when he will return as the Christ.

LORD MAITREYA

During that life, he will attain the great Initiation of the Buddha, and those who have been his students in past lives will gain perfect knowing, remembering Him, and they will all be strongly attracted towards Him. Under his influence great numbers of them will enter the Path, and many will advance to the higher stages, having already made considerable progress in previous incarnations. When Lord Maitreya is promoted to the position of The Buddha, currently being held by Lord Gautama, large numbers of prior students will instantly attain the Arhat level of the fourth initiation, which in Christian symbology is associated with the suffering in the garden of Gethsemane, the Crucifixion and the Resurrection of the Christ. The Lord Maitreya, at the time of Jesus's baptism in the river Jordan, "overlighted" Jesus to the end of his life.

Overlighting was a process of melding his consciousness from the spiritual world into the physical body and consciousness of Jesus. In a sense, they shared the same physical body during the last three years of Jesus' life, and most people do not realize this. Many of the miracles and sayings attributed to Jesus were really those of Lord Maitreya, who holds the position in the Spiritual Hierarchy called the Office of the Christ. Jesus so perfectly embodied the Christ Consciousness that it enabled Lord Maitreya, who is the Planetary Christ, to meld his consciousness with that of Jesus.

This great sacrifice and renunciation by Jesus, along with the crucifixion experience, earned Him the passing of his fourth initiation, which was his liberation from the wheel of rebirth. It was, in actuality, Lord Maitreya who, as the Christ Spirit, ascended in that lifetime and resurrected Jesus' physical body, not Jesus himself. The Lord Maitreya passed his sixth initiation at the crucifixion, and hence the prophecy of the second coming of the Christ really means both the second coming of the Lord Maitreya that was predicted 2,000 years ago as well as the second coming of the Christ Consciousness in all incarnated personalities on Earth.

The Christ Consciousness is the consciousness of the soul rather than the consciousness of the fear-based, separate, and selfish negative ego. The key here is that all are meant to embody the Christ Consciousness, meaning each person is the Christ. In truth, everyone has the potential to be like the Christ. It was not, and is not just Jesus or the Lord Maitreya who is the Christ. We all have that spark of God within us, because we all have a soul, which makes us a part of God. The other ascended masters are examples of how we can all raise our consciousness to the point of Ascension, and become a God-realized being, just as they are.

Lord Maitreya/the Christ Spirit is currently in a body of the Celtic race. His face is very beautiful, strong yet tender, with rich flowing hair the color of red gold about his shoulders. He has a pointed beard, and his eyes are a beautiful violet color, like sparkling flowers, like stars, or deep holy pools of water of everlasting life and peace. His smile is dazzling beyond words, and a blinding white Light surrounds Him, intermingled with a marvelous rose-colored glow that is always associated with Him.

The Christ Spirit is coming to finish the work He began 2,000 years ago. His message through Master Jesus has been negated, forgotten, or misinterpreted for 2,000 years, and hate and separation have entered into the situation. The generally accepted idea that He will return in the clouds as a triumphant warrior, omnipotent and irresistible, surely has no basis in fact. He will ultimately, lead His people — humanity — into Jerusalem (not the actual city of Jerusalem), into the place of peace, which is what the word Jerusalem means. He has again "set His face to go to Jerusalem," as it says in the Bible. He will reappear and guide humankind into a civilization and a state of consciousness, where right human relations, and worldwide co-operation for the good of all will be the universal keynote. He cares not what the faith is, if the objective is love of God and humanity. The Christ has no religious barriers in His consciousness. It does not matter to Him what faith a man may call himself.

In the Eastern teachings, Lord Maitreya/The Christ Spirit, embodied the Wisdom of God. He also brought Light and Love to its full expression, and He is now bringing the Will of God to humanity.

Many churches only emphasize the dying of Jesus Christ on the cross, instead of lifting up the living, working, active, present Christ, who has been with us. The church of today that Christ is looking for is finding expression in all people who love their fellow humans, in all people who see how they are all the same without restrictions or reservations. It is not the accepting of any historical fact or theological creed that places us en rapport with Christ. The members of the kingdom of God are all those who are deliberately seeking the light and attempting to stand before God and achieve ascension.

The work of the Christ is affected by certain phases of spiritual, and cyclic timing. He makes needed adjustments, and brings about change in a timely manner.

As evolution proceeds, people begin to understand that speech, the written word, and motivated activity are all expressions of energy, which leads to the spread of energy, and all activities that are expressions of energy cause its distribution. Energy can be spread by one person or by many, according to the thought, word, or deed being utilized. People will achieve power and expression, when they consciously use energy to produce good works. The Hierarchy is a great energy center, and through the Christ, its energy reaches humanity.

A great movement is taking place on the Earth, which will go on until 2025. At the great General Assembly of the Hierarchy in 2001, new impacts for humanity were put into place for the 21st Century. 2025 looks to be the first stage of the externalization of the Hierarchy.

MASTER KUTHUMI

MASTER KUTHUMI

One who is working very closely with the Christ Spirit is Master Kuthumi, who is in direct line to shortly become Chohan of the Second Ray. He will assume the scepter of the world teacher, the position Lord Maitreya currently holds, and become the Bodhisattva of the sixth root race in the future. He is working with education, giving understanding and wisdom through love. The Ray of love and wisdom gives great teachers to the world. The work is now proceeding under the direction of the Bodhisattva and the Buddha, who are directing Master Kuthumi and the other members who are working with this Ray.

Master Kuthumi wears the body of a Kashmiri Brahmin; he is tall, and fair of complexion, looking much like the average Englishman. His hair and beard are light brown, with glints of gold when seen in the sunlight. He has a finely chiseled nose, and large blue eyes that are illuminated from within, like a wonderful liquid blue. His face is somewhat hard to describe, because his expression is constantly changing as he smiles.

He radiates love and wisdom and displays much patience and understanding when teaching. He is transmuting the thoughts of religious beliefs, filling churches with the idea of the Coming of the Christ. He is bringing a suffering world the vision of a Great Helper — the Christ. He works with the great guardian angel Lord Varuna. Earth's activity is being intensified, and those who are connected with the divine light of good will are being worked with on higher levels to strengthen and redirect their spiritual aspiration and desire. The angels who work with these energies are increasing the momentum of their vibration to raise the consciousness of the congregation. Master Kuthumi also works with the leaders of the Catholic, Greek, Roman, and Anglican Churches. He works with the leaders and foremost workers in education. His interests lie with all those who have unselfish intent, those who strive for the ideal of oneness, and those who live to help others.

Lord Maitreya was Kuthumi's teacher, and he also trained with the Lord Maha Chohan, and the Divine Director, who taught him the exact instruction of the "I AM."

Kuthumi incarnated as the Greek philosopher Pythagoras around 500 to 600 B.C. He settled in Southern Italy at Crotona between 540 and 530 B.C., where he made many important discoveries in various studies such as mathematics, geometry, astronomy, and music. He determined that the world was round, and that the planets produced music of the spheres. He taught that the real self was immortal, and He came back into embodiment many times. He taught these doctrines at his school.

In another life, Kuthumi was Balthazar, one of the Wise Men, who followed the star to Jesus's birthplace. He could have ascended then, like El Morya, but He chose not to in order to have a closer physical connection to humanity to bring more information forward for the people on Earth.

Saint Francis of Assisi, who went out to preach in 1208 A.D., was another past life of Kuthumi. He was such a lover of nature, that he would watch a certain phase for hours, or he would spend a whole day with a flower to see it open into full bloom and perhaps watch it close again at night. He was one of the few who represented the heart of the nature kingdom. He could reach through the elemental kingdom and accelerate his own consciousness to a point where he was of assistance in that realm. Birds and animals were drawn to him to be in his radiance.

Kuthumi founded the Order of Franciscan Friars, the Order of St. Clara, and then a third called the Tertiaries. He built the Taj Mahal from 1630 to 1652 A.D., during another past life. The Taj Mahal is one of the world's most beautiful buildings, and Kuthumi built it for the woman he loved. It is said that when the marble is chipped off, it replaces itself automatically.

Kuthumi was at Oxford University around 1850 in his last lifetime, where he played a key role in popularizing Theosophy. In that life He was from India and lived for many years in a Himalayan valley with some of the other ascended masters. It was said that He maintained that body for 300 years and that He ascended around 1889.

Master El Morya

Ascended Master El Morya is Chohan of the First Ray and serves under the Manu, who heads the first department of the Hierarchy. The

MASTER EL MORYA

First Ray works directly with the Will of God. El Morya's role is as a representative of the Manu and the Hierarchy, who give assistance to all governments. He is ever standing by, ready to do God's will. Master El Morya will be the future Manu, or Ruler, of the sixth root race, about 500 years from now, which, as I mentioned, will be located in the California area.

El Morya has a dark beard divided into two parts, almost black; he wears his hair long, falling to his shoulders, and he has dark piercing eyes, full of power.

Sometimes he wears a white turban. He is 6' 6" tall, with the bearing of a soldier. He speaks in short, terse sentences, as if he were accustomed to being instantly obeyed. In his presence, there is a sense of overwhelming power and strength. He has an imperial dignity that compels the deepest reverence.

Currently, Master El Morya is inspiring great business people all over the world. Those who work with vision and hold the ideal of oneness are under His supervision. He is working for the world to continue becoming more international in its thinking, with all people working together in oneness. He seeks to touch the third-eye center of all intuitive statesmen. Master El Morya is working with three groups of angels — the gold, the flame colored, and the white and gold. These angels are working on mental levels with other angels who energize thoughts, who protect the thoughts of the race for the benefit of humanity.

Most of El Morya's past lives were masculine, and he has been a king a number of times. He was Melchior, one of the three wise men who found their way to the Christ Child. He could have ascended then, but He refused it, in order to help bring forth Theosophy, which would not have been possible from the ascended state. El Morya, Kuthumi, and Djwhal Khul tried through Theosophy to bring the understanding to humanity concerning the truth about life, telling them there is no death, but humankind was not able at that time to understand the concept.

Theosophy acquainted truth seekers in the west with the masters. Here the three worked together again, as they are also doing at present. Their twin Rays, or divine complements, are in physical bodies, rendering service to humankind at this time, under the guidance of the Great White Brotherhood.

El Morya led three crusades and was King Arthur in the fifth and sixth centuries. He incarnated as Thomas Moore in 1478 in England and is responsible for the poems by Sir Thomas Moore, the Irish poet. He purposely wrote poetry to soften his nature to gain balance against the many embodiments of rulership.

Hercules was El Morya's teacher, and he also received training under the Maha Chohan. El Morya was a Rajput prince in India, and it was said He retained that body for 325 years, before he ascended around 1888.

Ascended master El Morya worked with Madame Helena P. Blavatsky from the latter part of the 19th century through the early part of the 20th century. Blavatsky established the first dispensation of the spiritual Hierarchy's teachings through Master El Morya in books and made the information available to humanity.

Master Djwhal Khul

Another ascended master working closely with the Christ Spirit at this time is the Tibetan Djwhal Khul (D.K.), who was also known as Gai Benjamin in his youth in the early part of the 20th century. This life occurred before He became an adept (fifth-degree initiate). He is often referred to as the Master D.K., or as "The Tibetan."

Master Djwhal Khul is still wearing the same body in which he attained adeptship. His face is distinctly Tibetan in character, with high cheek bones, and He is somewhat rugged in appearance, showing signs of age. He has grey hair with a receding hairline, and very penetrating golden-brown eyes. He has a Roman nose with flaring nostrils, and he wears a mustache. He has a well-shaped mouth with full lips, and olive-colored skin.

The Master Djwhal Khul works closely with Lord Maitreya and Master Kuthumi on the Second Ray. He helps those who deal with pure altruism. He occupies Himself with those who are active in the

MASTER DJWHAL KHUL

laboratories of the world, with great philanthropic world movements like the Red Cross, and with the rapidly developing social-service movements. His work also embraces teaching, and He does much at this time to train various disciples in this hour of crisis, by giving them teaching responsibilities to help humankind. Many of the healing angels, like those referred to in the Bible, cooperate with Him.

Djwhal Khul was Confucius in the 6th century B.C., in China, and I was his student, editing and compiling sacred writings. The essence of Confucianism is to strive for perfect virtue in every thought, word, and deed. He believed that all people are basically good at heart and that salvation could be achieved through this essential nature. His most important contribution was in ethics, and his proverbs are quoted to this day.

Djwhal Khul was on Lemuria before the continent sank, and he accompanied Lord Himalaya as he took the treasures to the heart of Asia for safekeeping. He embodied many times in the mountains of Asia, where he lived in the great Lamaseries. He was Kleinias, Pythagoras's favorite pupil and the first chela (student) of Lord Gautama Buddha. It is claimed that he was also Aryasanga, who translated into English the Sutras of Patanjali, by Shankaracharya. He later gave an English paraphrase of them to Alice A. Bailey.

He worked with El Morya and Kuthumi, bringing forth Theosophy. He was devoted to Kuthumi, and built Himself a small house up the ravine from Kuthumi's home at Shigatse, Tibet. He willingly served in any capacity, doing whatever there was to be done, and through such service acquired the name "The Messenger of the Masters." It seems He always preferred to stay in the background and avoid outer recognition as much as possible. He dictated a large part of Madame Blavatsky's *The Secret Doctrine*. He manifested from thin air several pictures during those days of Theosophy.

Djwhal Khul, like El Morya and Kuthumi, the other two Wise Men, presumably could have ascended at the close of that embodiment, but chose not to complete it then, in order to also have a closer physical connection for the future service with Theosophy. He attained mastery, just as El Morya and Kuthumi had, to the point of suddenly appearing in a room without the door opening, seemingly out of the atmosphere.

He became an adept (ascended master) on the second Ray of love/wisdom, in the latter part of the 19th century. Djwhal Khul secured a dispensation to give information to humankind through his work with Alice A. Bailey. He persuaded her to take it, and he wrote quite a bit of it to convince her of its quality. She consented to do the work, and the door was opened for the ascended masters to reach humanity once again. Much more law and spiritual understanding has been given since then.

The work had already been laid out at inner levels when Mrs. Bailey started to take it in 1919; soon after the 30 years of work was done in 1949, she departed from this world, having completed her service. The work brought in a new and wider field, including group work, particularly on the inner levels. Up to this time, teaching of this kind had only been obtainable to the students by accepting their teacher's authority through oaths and pledges. The relationship between the student and the master remains the same, but this information has brought more spiritual understanding. The work progressed to a new level, and student training began to be presented through group action, bringing New Age training forward into the 20th century.

Djwhal Khul is more familiar with the working of the Hierarchy and the Rays than any of the other masters. He is in charge of organized thought and wisdom, and he is an authority on cycles.

I have been working closely with Master Djwhal Khul for many years, and he has been of great assistance putting this book together. It was revealed to me that I was his student in a past life, when I visited Mt. Shasta, California, in August of 2006. Later that year He told me that I was to write a book. Some of the information in this book has been written in the words it was given, which might sound more like an ancient form of communication.

Master Hilarion

Ascended Master Hilarion is actively working in America at this time, stimulating the intuitive perception of the people. He is the

MASTER HILARION

Chohan of the Fifth Ray, with his splendid quality of scientific accuracy. He influences most of the great scientists of the world, and people who are well advanced along his Ray are notable for their ability to make accurate observations. They are absolutely dependable where scientific investigation is concerned. His field of abilities extends well beyond the scientific arena, into the realms of nature. He works with many of the forces of Nature and introduces aspects of Nature into the lives of people. He observes all the true psychics who develop their powers for the good of the community.

Master Hilarion controls and transmutes the great active movement that is stripping the veil from the world of the unseen. He has much to do with various psychical research movements throughout the world. With the aid of certain groups of angels, he is working to open up the other side of departed souls to the seeker. He is helping to bring more attention to these areas, so the people will understand what happens to our souls after we die.

Hilarion was a priest in the Temple of Truth on Atlantis, and he was part of a group who took the Flame of Truth and some documents to Greece shortly before Atlantis sank, thereby preserving the Flame of Truth for the Earth. He established the Focus of Truth in Greece for the future of humankind. Later the Oracles of Delphi were established, and the initiates were directed by the Flame of Truth for hundreds of years. Great Truth came forth during that time period. Later on, some priests came into the Temple of Truth who were not very pure and selfless, and they brought in impure forces, which caused the corruption and destruction of the Temple. The people no longer had faith in the Delphic Order, and it reached the point where the masters had to withdraw, and the Flame of Truth could no longer be used to bring forth wisdom.

Hilarion was in Tibet in the latter part of the 1800s along with some other ascended masters, including Lord Maitreya, Kuthumi, St. Germain, Djwhal Khul, and El Morya. Hilarion incarnated as John the Beloved, a disciple of Jesus. He has mistakenly been identified with the disciple Paul via some writings today, but according to Djwhal Khul, Hilarion was the John who wrote the Book of Revelations over 1900 years ago. He also embodied as Lamblichus, of the Neoplatonic School.

Hilarion assists the agnostics, skeptics, atheists, and the spiritually disappointed and disillusioned to have faith in God. This work is being done on the inner levels, as well as in those still in physical form. He has great persuasive power and is very successful instilling renewed faith in God. Hilarion and his group help people cross over to the other side at their passing. They can take them to the Temple of Truth, where they especially assist the non-believers in the hereafter. He assists anyone who desires it to know the Truth.

People who believe in vicarious atonement find out, when they have passed to the other side, that it is not as represented on Earth. Experiences such as these cause disillusion in people who are sincerely seeking the truth. When they are misled and become disappointed, a record of this is created in the etheric body, producing disbelief and skepticism.

Master Hilarion also consecrates people of all seven Rays who have a vocation. He also enjoys working on research in the medical profession. Healing is one of His main activities, and it is one of the things He is best known for today. He has many responsibilities as Chohan of the Fifth Ray for the Great White Brotherhood.

Master Serapis Bey

Ascended Master Serapis Bey is the Chohan of the Fourth Ray. He is very active today helping the Lord of Civilization, St. Germain, bring in the energy of the seventh Ray for the Aquarian Age. His body is Greek by birth, though all his work has been done in Egypt in connection with the Egyptian Lodge. He is tall and fair in complexion, very distinguished, ascetic in face, and his eyes are amber colored. He has been helping bring about constructive work to help humanity. He conceived the idea of world unity in the realm of politics, which worked out as the intelligent banding together of nations for the preservation of international peace. He presented this plan to the nations of the world, including the ascended masters of the Hierarchy.

MASTER SERAPIS BEY

He felt strongly that something could be done. This occurred when Woodrow Wilson was president of the United States, and the plan was passed on to Col. House, who had the president's ear. It was then presented to the world as the League of Nations.

Master Serapis Bey is the great disciplinarian known throughout the centuries for maintaining strict behavior concerning disciplines relating to ascension. These disciplines must be learned and practiced at all times. He came as a guardian to help with the evolution of the Earth, and took physical embodiment to be of assistance to the Hierarchy. He also works with the Seraphim kingdom.

He was a priest in the Ascension Temple on Atlantis before it sank, and he was given the task of taking a portion of the Ascension Flame to safety. He along with 40 of the Brotherhood sailed to Egypt. Just after landing on the Nile near Luxor, they became aware of the sinking of Atlantis by the rumble and shaking of the Earth.

He established a Temple of the Ascension Flame, and he has been the guardian of that Flame ever since. Some trusted Brother in physical body would stand guard when Serapis Bey was at inner levels in between lives. Since the sinking of Atlantis around 12,000 years ago, nearly all of his past lives have been in Egypt, during which time he built the temples at Thebes and Karnak.

Serapis Bey incarnated as King Leonidas of Sparta and was well known for discipline at that time. He assisted with the creation of the Colossus at Rhodes during a past life in Greece. He incarnated as Phidias in Athens, where he mostly worked as an architect and sculptor. He designed the Parthenon and supervised its construction until it was completed.

He made his ascension around 400 B.C., and shortly after became Chohan of the Fourth Ray, working with harmony and beauty. The Fourth Ray is the dominant Ray of the greater cycle, along with the Seventh Ray of ceremonial magic.

Ascended Master Jesus

After Jesus ascended into heaven He later came back to Earth in subsequent lives, according to ascended master Djwhal Khul. He

ASCENDED MASTER JESUS

returned to the Earth again as Apollonius of Tyana very soon after His death as Jesus. In his life of Apollonius, at the age of 12, he was sent to study literature, rhetoric, and all forms of philosophy. He was initiated in the city of Tarsus into the healing arts in the temple of Aesculapius. He committed himself to following the philosophy of Pythagoras. He became a vegetarian, abstaining from alcohol, and from all sexual activity. He dressed only in a white robe, and he walked barefoot. His handsome features are said to have resembled those of Jesus; he had a long beard and hair to his shoulders. Apollonius committed himself to the pursuit of knowledge and philosophy. He gave his money to his poor relatives and traveled to Antioch, where he began receiving disciples and teaching. He studied in the temple of Apollo, and later traveled to India and Egypt in search of knowledge. His travels were similar to those he took as Jesus. He traveled the world counseling, teaching, and helping others. He had great modesty and virtue, and at one point in his life, he was imprisoned and sentenced to death. He used his brilliant oratory skills at his trial, and secured his own freedom. Apollonius spread the Eastern teachings along with his foundation in the Grecian mysteries of Orpheus and Pythagoras. On his return to Greece, he was regarded as a divine personage with miraculous powers. At the advanced age of 100 years, he disappeared without leaving a trace.

Jesus came back one more time in the 1600s in a Syrian body and lived in the Holy Land. He traveled much of the time, and spent a considerable amount of time in various parts of Europe. He was rather a martial figure, a disciplinarian, and a man of iron rule and will. In the Syrian body, He was tall and spare, rather a long thin face, black hair, pale complexion and piercing blue eyes.

He is in charge of the Sixth Ray of Devotion at this time in the Hierarchy, working with the ascended masters to bring about the necessary changes for the Aquarian Age. He is steering the thoughts of people out of its present state of war into the peaceful waters of love and knowledge. He is preparing the way in Europe and America for the eventual coming of the new world teacher. His work on the sixth Ray has to do with the Christian Church, helping to bring the true spiritual life forward, and to neutralize, as much as possible, the mistakes and errors of the churchmen and the theologians. He works closely with the Christ in church matters, and He helps to bring forward all that is best in the Christian teachings.

MASTER PAUL

MASTER PAUL THE VENETIAN

Master Paul the Venetian is a Master of the Third Ray, and he is working closely with the Maha Chohan, St. Germain, The Master St. Germain heads the Third Ray Department as Maha Chohan, and Lord of Civilization at this time. St. Germain is also in charge of Rays 3, 4, 5, 6, and 7. His responsibilities are vast and much depends on the actions that are taken at this time.

Master Paul is working as acting head of the Third Ray to help St. Germain with his vast responsibilities. He is working closely with the Christ and inner circle of ascended masters to help bring enlightenment to the world.

Paul the Venetian is believed to have been incarnated as a "Minister of Culture" in the government of Atlantis. He was one of the architects of the pyramids in ancient Egypt. He was an artist (mural painter) in the Inca Empire. He is believed to have ascended on April 19, 1588.

C.W. Leadbeater, in *Masters On The Path* mentions a Venetian Chohan, but did not name him Paul or identify him with Veronese (whom some say was a past life of Paul).

12

Sri Sathya Sai Baba

SRI SATHYA SAI BABA

One of the greatest and most glorious beings recently on Earth was Sri Sathya Sai Baba, who lived in India. He was an avatar, a God-realized being at birth. An avatar does not have to do any spiritual practices to attain self-realization. Avatars are already self-realized at birth. The miracles that Jesus performed in the last three years of his life, including raising the dead, turning water into wine, and walking on water, have been done by Sai Baba ever since his birth.

Sai Baba's coming was foretold over 5,000 years ago in one of the holiest books in India, the Mahabharata, in which Vishnu, who is part of the Hindu trinity of Brahma, Vishnu, and Shiva, foretells of a future age of decline called the Kali Yuga. We are now in that age, and it was at its lowest ebb in 500 A.D. We were going through the Dark Ages at that time, and we are now ascending out of the Kali Yuga period, according to Sai Baba.

When the age of darkness was still lingering on the Earth, Vishnu foretold that He would return to Earth as a great spiritual being — an avatar. The Mahabharata gave certain characteristics concerning the coming avatar — he would be short with a blood-red robe; he would bear the name Truth (Sathya means truth in Hindi); he would have a triple-avatar incarnation; and he would be born in southern India with the avatar's birthmark on the bottom of his foot. His parents would be worshipers of Krishna, and the child would be divine, and fully God-realized. He would be all-knowing and the greatest living being in the world. He would be able to lengthen life and be in many places at once. Good would come to anyone who saw him.

All of these prophecies given over 5,000 years ago perfectly describe Sai Baba. Once a person was exposed to the love of Sai Baba's auric field, and his magic presence, they were never the same again. It is said that his auric field was over 1,000 miles in diameter.

Over the years many wonderful stories have been written about the things Sai Baba did for people. At 13, he was bitten by a scorpion and lost consciousness for 24 hours. When he awoke, his family was gathered all around him, and he told them that in a past life he had been the great avatar, Shirdi Sai Baba. His family didn't believe him, so he picked up a vase of flowers and threw it on the ground. They flew all over the place, and when the flowers had settled on the ground they spelled out the words "Shirdi Sai Baba." Shirdi Sai Baba was born in the late 1800s and lived into the early 1900s.

Shortly after this happened, he told his family, "My devotees are waiting for me. I am leaving home for good." Sai Baba then left his home and began his ashram.

As Sathya Sai Baba, he said that when he died in his last life as Sai Baba, he would pass into the spirit world and then reincarnate two years later as Prema Sai Baba. He has told his devotees that he would return, and he has materialized a picture of himself in his future life as Prema Sai Baba.

Sai Baba said that in his life as Shirdi Sai Baba, he was the incarnation of the Shiva, or father energy. In his recent life as Sathya Sai Baba, he was the incarnation of both the Shiva and the Shakti, or mother energy, and in his next life as Prema Sai Baba, he will be carrying the Shakti energy.

He materialized whatever he wanted instantly with just the swirl of his hand, and he did this whenever he felt the need to do so. Many books have been written by him and about him by his devotees. Videos are also available in which you can see him materialize objects.

In 1998 I traveled to India to see Sai Baba with a small group of people. We stayed at his ashram for two weeks. During this time we would get up each morning, and go to meditation. As I was meditating one morning, I asked Sai Baba to heal my tongue that had been numb on the left side since an auto accident in 1991. I had not been able to feel food on that side of my tongue when I ate, and the doctor said it was from cranial nerve damage and that it would never get any better. Right after I asked Sai Baba to heal me, my tongue started tingling, which continued until the next day. For the first time since the accident, I could feel the food in my mouth, on the side of my tongue that had been numb for seven years.

To sit in his presence was one of the most loving experiences I have ever encountered. Many people traveled from all over the world to see him. Sai Baba had devotees all over the world, and a large number were from the United States.

Mr. and Mrs. Walter Cowan were traveling in India one day, when Walter died from a heart attack in a city far from Sai Baba's ashram. Mrs. Cowan tried to contact Sai Baba by telegram but couldn't get hold of him. Six or eight hours later, Sai Baba received the telegram, and suddenly appeared at the hospital. Mr. Cowan's friends and family had already left the hospital. Sai Baba asked to see Mr. Cowan's body, and he was left alone with it. Five minutes later, Sai Baba walked out with Mr. Cowan totally alive and able to walk out of the hospital just fine on his own. The doctors were astounded.

Then Walter went to see his wife and family, and they were totally shocked. He told his wife and family that when he died, Sai Baba was there with him in the spirit world. Sai Baba had taken him to a council chamber filled with people gathered around the chairman of the council, who read out loud all of Walter's past lives for two hours, after which Sai Baba said to the chairman that Walter had not yet completed his mission on Earth and that he wanted to take him back to his physical body so he could complete his mission. The chairman gave his permission, and Sai Baba took Walter back to his physical body, where he awoke next to Sai Baba!

He brought another devotee back to life who had been dead for over 72 hours, and Sai Baba arrived and gave one of his divine orders, much as Jesus did when he said, "Lazarus, arise!" The man awoke after having been dead for over three days! Sai Baba gave him some hot tea, which the man drank. Sai Baba then told him that he should go and comfort his family, for they were worried about him,.

Once Sai Baba was lecturing a group of students at a school he started, telling them about an emerald necklace that Krishna had worn in his life 7,000 years ago. All of a sudden Sai Baba said, "Would you like to see this emerald necklace?" With a wave of his hand he materialized Krishna's necklace and passed it around the room for the students to see and touch. After everyone had examined it, he sent it back to where it had come from, with another wave of his hand.

Sai Baba said that there are 16 signs by which an avatar can be known. They are control of the five functions of the body, the five senses of the body, and the elements of nature. These first 15 are attainable through spiritual practice and spiritual disciplines. The 16th quality, Sai Baba says, is attainable only by the descent of a divine Incarnation — an avatar who is God-realized at birth with absolute omniscience, omnipresence, and omnipotence.

Sai Baba never slept, and when someone asked him why he performed miracles, he said that he did it to get people's attention in order to turn them toward God. His Virbutti ash, which he created with a wave of his hand, is used for healing purposes and as a blessing.

He said that he is not here to create a new religion, but rather to repair the ancient ways of understanding God. His recommendation is for people to keep whatever religion they are affiliated with. He will come to any sincere request for God, regardless of the form, for he says all forms are One in reality. He said, "There is only one religion — the religion of love. There is only one language — the language of the heart. There is only one race — the race of humanity. There is only one God, and He is omnipresent." He said, the thing to understand is that everyone is God — the Christ, the Buddha, the Atma, and the Eternal Self, and that all should see themselves this way and see each person they meet this way, for how one treats each person one meets is how one treats Him. He said, "God equals man minus ego," and that ego is the illusion of separation, fear, and selfishness. He also said, "Hands that help are holier than lips that pray."

Sai Baba often stated that "A guru is the Light to show one the road, but the destination is God. One is grateful to one's guru, but it is God that one worships. Nowadays one worships the guru, which is quite wrong."

He gave people wonderful advice on how to live — "Start the day with love. Fill the day with love. Spend the day with love. And end the day with love, for this is the way to God."

Sai Baba passed into the other realms April 24, 2011, at age 96, the age he said he would die....

THE DEPARTMENT OF THE WORLD MOTHER...

There is another department that has the World Mother, more commonly known as Mother Mary, the Mother of Jesus at its head. She has vast hosts of angelic beings at her command. She is now filling the post of World Mother, who looks after the mothers of the world when they are ready to give birth. The duty of this department is to look after every woman in the time of her suffering, to give her such help and strength as her karma allows.

At the birth of every child one of these angels is always present as the World Mother's representative. She is present at the bedside of every mother through her representative. Many women have seen her under such conditions, and many who have not been privileged to see her, have felt her help and strength. It is the desire of the World Mother that every woman be enfolded in deep and true affection, at the time of her delivery. The expectant mother should be filled with the holiest and noblest thoughts, so none but the highest influences may be brought to bear upon the child to be born. When we keep our thoughts positive, it helps give the child a healthy start in life.

It is very important that women be careful of the way they care for themselves, for the benefit of the children before, during, and after their pregnancy. Perfect cleanliness, and strict attention should be paid to their thoughts, keeping love, happiness, and holiness present at the birth. In this way, the future of the race will be assured, and we will be of great assistance to the work of Mother Mary, and the angels. The World Mother requests that every birth be treated with special care.

She was chosen to be the Mother of Jesus long ago in Palestine, because of her wonderful quality of intense purity, and soul development. She displayed patience and nobility of soul, and bore all the terrible suffering, which came to her as the consequences of that position. She attained the level of Adeptship (Ascension) in that same life. Once we reach ascension, we find different paths before us to choose from and she chose to enter the glorious Deva (Angel) evolution. She was received into this position with great honor and respect. A great Deva or angel needs no physical body; while she holds her present office, she will always appear to us in feminine form. The other angels who are helping her with her work are also in feminine form.

Through the centuries many people have poured devotion at her feet. Her love of humankind has evoked it, and it has been used in the onerous task she has undertaken. She has been honored and received the prayers of many people asking for help throughout the years since her death. Not only is she the Mother of Jesus, but she is also recognized as the symbol of Motherhood for all living people all over the world. The World Mother is recognized in China as Kwan-Yin, in India as Jagat-Amba, and in other parts of the world under different names. She is essentially the representative, the very type of essence of love, devotion, and purity. Most important of all, she is the counselor, comforter, and helper of all who are in trouble, sorrow, sickness, or need.

The truth that lies behind the Roman Catholic doctrine of her Assumption, is not that she was carried into heaven among the angels in her physical body. It happened when she left that body and ascended, taking her place among the angels. She is presently appointed to the office of World Mother, truly a queen among the angels, as the church so poetically says. Mother Mary is playing a huge role in the world today. She is taking a very active part now in helping to bring Christ back to the Earth. Throughout the 20th Century she has been showing up in different ways all over the world, doing her part to bring humanity back to the Light.

Feminine energy is becoming more powerful now, due to the beginning of the New Age. Many women are beginning to channel Mother Mary, and information is being given to warn mankind of coming times. She has been warning us to prepare for the days ahead, and many people have been receiving these messages. She appeared at

Fatima, Portugal to three children many years ago. In the days ahead, the feminine energy will keep growing stronger on the Earth and Mother Mary energy will be getting more powerful. The people who are in tune with this energy will be able to receive messages.

In some of the oldest holy books, the Holy Ghost is definitely mentioned as being feminine. In the cycle before this one in Atlantis, the feminine energy was the strongest and we have just gone through the masculine energy of this age. Maybe in the Aquarian Age just beginning, we will be responsible to balance our male and female energy. In Atlantis, some of the most advanced souls were androgynous, with both male and female together in one body. When our vibration became lower, we were separated from our twin soul into two bodies, as is spoken of in the Bible, when a rib was said to be taken from Adam's body to create Eve in the Garden of Eden.

13
St. Germain — Maha Chohan, Lord Of Civilization

ASCENDED MASTER ST. GERMAIN

Since St. Germain is head of the third department of the Great White Brotherhood, he is in charge of the fourth, fifth, sixth, and seventh rays of the Hierarchy. He has responsibilities, especially at this time, involving the people of the world. Known as the Lord of

Civilization, the Maha Chohan, and he is over the department of Active Intelligence and works with the leaders of the other two departments that make up the Inner Council, who work directly with the Christ Spirit. He takes the general plan, as outlined by the Inner Council Chamber and takes appropriate action to bring it into being on Earth. He might be regarded as the general manager, carrying out the plans of the executive council of the Christ Spirit. He has a vast amount of power and authority with the Hierarchy.

St. Germain is in charge of preparing the activities on Earth and is responsible for assisting humanity to move forward in evolution at this time. He is involved with every area that affects humanity from culture, institutions, education, and styles of living, to sexual relations.

Our society must be changed on all levels, to bring it forward into the Aquarian Age because of the new energies coming in at this time, which will change everything as we know it.

When St. Germain assumed the task of Maha Chohan, his students were shifted from the seventh Ray to the third Ray of Active Intelligence. Most of those who have taken the second and third initiations were transferred with him under what might be called a "special dispensation." The rest of his students remained for tuition and training in service under the master who took his place.

St. Germain is not especially tall, but he has a very upright, military bearing. He has the exquisite courtesy and dignity of a grand seigneur of the 18th century. While in his presence, we can feel that He belongs to a very old and noble family. His has large, brown eyes filled with tenderness and humor, although you can detect a glint of power in them at certain times. The splendor of His presence impels people to make obeisance. His face is olive-tan skin, his close-cut brown hair is parted in the center and brushed back from the forehead. He has a short, pointed beard. He often wears a dark uniform with facings of gold lace, and sometimes he wears a magnificent red military cloak. He has a suit of golden chain mail, which once belonged to a Roman Emperor, and over it is thrown a magnificent crimson cloak, fastened with a clasp displaying an amethyst and a seven-pointed star of diamonds. St. Germain sometimes wears a glorious violet robe. He usually resides in an ancient castle in Eastern Europe that belonged to his family for centuries.

St. Germain does not take as many students as the other masters do at this time. He currently handles most of the third-Ray students in America with Master Hilarion and works mainly through the seventh-Ray energy of ceremonial magic and order, which includes the ceremonies of the Freemasons, various fraternities, and churches everywhere. He is called "the Count" in the Great White Brotherhood, and he carries out the plans of the executive council in both America and Europe.

Because we are now in the fifth sub-root race of the fifth root race, the pressure of the work on the five Rays controlled by the Maha Chohan is very great. Shortly, the sixth root race will begin the many changes in store that must be completed in order to bring in the new root race.

The destiny of the world lies in the hands of the three groups of initiated disciples and the Chohan Masters, who are in charge of them. Masters El Morya, Kuthumi, and St. Germain are moving toward a period of intense activity, and it is very important that everyone attuned to these masters work with them to help bring in the Aquarian Age. As the people help to bring in the Divine Plan, and cooperate with these masters and their groups, new opportunities will emerge. The triangle of energy created by the masters of the three departments is held up by the great leaders in Shamballa, to help regulate world affairs.

Three other masters who are under the direction of St. Germain are Masters Hilarion, Serapis Bey, and Jesus, all of whom are assisting with the major task of bring in this new energy of the seventh Ray. Prior to the coming of the Christ, adjustments will be made to put either a master or an initiate who has taken the third initiation, at the head of certain groups, like the Freemasons and various Church divisions.

Masters and initiates will be found in many great nations of the world. This work is moving forward now, and the group of ascended masters, along with the initiates, are all working to bring the plan to a successful conclusion.

The masters are gathering those who show a tendency to respond to high vibration in any way, seeking to raise their frequencies to fit them in, so they may be of use at the time of the coming of the Christ. It will be a great day of opportunity when that time comes, through the wondrous strength of the vibration brought to bear on humanity. It will be possible for those who are now doing the necessary work to take a great step forward and to pass through the portal of initiation.

After the initial contact by Master St. Germain through the seventh Ray, we will see the unfolding of group awareness and loving understanding. This energy will be increased, making us more conscious of reality through inner development. When we look within to raise our awareness, we are moving toward the light of understanding. Once this occurs, we are ready to move outward toward our monad, or group.

St. Germain has lived many important lives in the past. He was Joseph, the husband of Mother Mary; He was Columbus, the explorer; He was Francis Bacon, who wrote all the plays of William Shakespeare. He was Merlin in King Arthur's court and the Jewish prophet Samuel. He was the son of Queen Elizabeth I, who never acknowledged him, but his true name was Francis Tudor, heir to the throne of England, although he was forced to use the name Francis Bacon. He was also Prince Rakoczy, a Hungarian with a home in the Carpathian Mountains, and he was once a well-known figure in the Hungarian Court.

Other assumed names of St. Germain include Christopher Marlowe, Edmund Spencer, Montaigne, Robert Burton, Cervantes, Andreas, and Comte de Gabalis.

It is believed that St. Germain was born in Hungary in 1561, as the Comte de St. Germain. He spoke all the European languages fluently without any foreign accent and was one of the best swordsmen of his day. He was a master violinist, with extraordinary powers of mind and a photographic memory. He could write two letters simultaneously, one by each hand, and each copy would be identical to the other, when held up to the light!

St. Germain's dream was to create in America a new country free of corruption, greed, and dictatorial monarchies. He was the father of modern democracy in America. He was instrumental in formulating the Declaration of Independence and the Constitution of the United States of America, as they were being written by his Masonic followers, who founded this nation. George Washington, Benjamin Franklin, Thomas Jefferson, and other founders were Freemasons, and their Masonic symbols can be seen on the dollar bill.

One lesser-known service that St. Germain performed was his translation of the King James Bible.

He traveled extensively in Europe and was known by all the royalty of that time period. He was personally known by Louis XVI, and Queen Marie Antoinette. Had they heeded his advice during the French Revolution, it would have saved their lives and many others as well.

He gave the elixir of life to several people, restoring their youth and beauty. He instructed and assisted Mesmer, was known by Cagliostro, exhibited alchemy to Cassanova, and assisted Charles of Hesse in the study of the secret sciences.

It was not generally known that St. Germain was an ascended being at that time, but everyone he met was in awe of his many abilities. He hoped to influence the people by creating whatever jewels, ornamentation, alchemy, or wealth they desired. He used this influence to catch the ears of the Kings and Queens, in order to help the Hierarchy direct events in the right direction for setting up the next stage of the work.

St. Germain knew Napoleon intimately and taught and trained him. He actually was the power behind him, as long as he respected him. St. Germain withdrew when Napoleon claimed the higher power as his own; and at that point, his failures began. St. Germain expected to make a United States of Europe through Napoleon, but again his efforts failed because of human weakness. St. Germain was a friend of Frederick the Great, and He had a hand in placing Catherine the Great upon Russia's throne. He was known to von Steuben, and influenced him to come to America. General Washington, Lafayette, and Franklin all knew him, as did Lincoln later. They knew him, but did not know that he was an ascended being. He fired up the patriots and swayed the signers of the Declaration of Independence into signing the document.

They looked for St. Germain later, but they could not find him, even though the doors were locked, and a man was on guard. He was an inspiration and power behind the bringing forth of the Magna Carta in England. It was through his endeavors that George Washington became the first President of the United States of America.

He was a power behind the building of trains, railroads, steamboats, airplanes, and suspension bridges, most of which he had predicted as Roger Bacon. He was also responsible for much of the lovely Austrian and Venetian music of the time. He inspired musicians like Chopin, Tchaikovsky, and Johann Strauss.

When he ceased working in Europe in the physical body, he said he would again be seen in 85 years, which was around the time that Theosophy emerged. He worked with Godfrey Ray King in the 1930s on Mt. Shasta, Calif., to bring forth the "I AM" teachings.

St. Germain become Chohan of the Seventh Ray around 100 years after his ascension, which was after his work in the Court of France and other parts of Europe, and after America's freedom, when he worked closely with people in the physical realm. When He assumed the Office of Chohan, his service entered the cosmic level, and He was no longer permitted to work in such close personal contact with people as before, except with Napoleon.

St. Germain was a priest in the Temples of Purification and the Violet Flame on Atlantis. He then received training on inner levels on divine alchemy in Archangel Zadkiel's temples over Cuba for centuries after Atlantis sank, until he became qualified to become guardian of the Violet Flame and the Chohan of the Seventh Ray.

He is the Director of the Transmuting Violet Flame to the Earth and therefore works as an angel deva of the violet flame, with legions of Angels under his direction. St. Germain took responsibility for securing dispensations for his students and humankind.

This is a special time to be in body on this planet, due to the many opportunities being offered to anyone who shows the desire to know more about the ascended masters and the Great White Brotherhood. The Transition into the sixth root race is the next step in the evolution of humanity, for which the Great White Brotherhood is recruiting many people all over the world. It certainly would be in our best interests to learn more about the ascended masters.

One thing you can be eternally certain of is that no one who is a real master will ever say that He/she is. Nor will an ascended master ever accept payment of any kind for helping others. The first qualification of true mastership is to do all that can be done with gladness and to be of service to others and the world.

Ascended masters are absolutely infallible at all times, because they have passed out of the lower vibrations, where mistakes can occur. They have become wholly divine, changing the cells of their bodies into pure light, as they went through the ascension process, and once this process was completed, they became immortal.

As we come to the end of the fifth race, and begin the New Age, we will see many events happening in the world creating catastrophic Earth changes, which will bring about mass migrations in the coming years.

In the next 200 years, we will see many new technological inventions that will assist us in making the needed changes to move forward in the world, and we can call on the ascended masters to help us find ways to be of service at that time.

St. Germain is utilizing the seventh-Ray energy, in order for people to recognize the subtle energies around us, and make us more attentive to our intuition and consciousness. Increased awareness will be brought about by the gradual opening of the third eye and by arousing the activity of the center at the base of the spine, the three channels in the spinal column, and the pineal gland.

This is the beginning of a new race of people on the Earth, and there will be some destruction of the old paradigms, to bring in changes that are needed for humanity to proceed on their evolutionary path. A part of the changes expected are the liberation of Spirit from constricting forms, blending Spirit and matter together. Serious disturbance may be looked for in the world, in order to bring in the changes to civilization that are called for at this time.

One of the main areas of change that is happening now is the bringing together of negative and positive aspects of natural processes like marriage bonds and sexual relationships of all forms. Some of the ways in which this energy is manifesting in the world include the creation of fundamental sexual problems, like promiscuity, problems in marriage relations, and divorce. These changes will eventually produce a new attitude towards sex and sexual practices. We will see more changes in marriage and moral perceptions that govern sexual relations in the Aquarian Age, which will help raise the lower vibrations and self-serving desires associated with sexual relations at this time to a higher vibrational level, changing the whole process for humanity. The sexual act must be raised from the lower chakras to the higher chakras, creating a higher vibrational energy. Currently, we are seeing much suffering and tragedy associated with the changes occurring in marriages.

During the next 100 years, we will see great changes in the marriage laws. The present laxity will inevitably bring a reaction, and the laws will become more stringent, in order to safeguard the race during the transition period. These laws will not allow young people to get married hastily, and it will not be as easy to escape a bad marriage. The rising generation will be properly instructed to be more discriminating about finding a mate.

Another angle of the Maha Chohan's work is connected with "sound," and how it affects our bodies. We are made up of different vibrations sensitive to different frequencies of sound, and these electromagnetic waves can be of a positive or negative nature. Humankind has created many harmful sounds like those of the great cities, manufacturing plants, and the weapons of war, all of which served to create a serious condition on Earth, which has to be offset in some way.

The future efforts of civilization will be directed towards educating the people to recycle, create non-polluting cars, use clean energy, and "go green." We are making great strides in this direction, and new technology will move humankind's future along in this direction. One of the main interests in the future will be eliminating destructive sounds, because we are becoming more sensitive to their effects on us.

The major weapon now being used by the combined forces of evil is chaos, disruption, and fear from lack of security. The potency of these evil forces is exceedingly great, because they belong to no particular group of people, and represent all kinds of belief systems. This chaos is produced by indifference, uncertainty, fear, starvation, war, conflict and watching innocent others suffer.

The general thinking in the world has to change, and that is a slow, arduous task. The evil personalities have to be replaced by those who can work in cooperation with St. Germain and his group, who are creating rhythm and beauty for the Aquarian Age.

In every nation, people tend to hold onto the old ways of the past, whether they are good or bad, then others work for a new point of view. Under the influence of energy coming in at this time, a balance will be achieved, creating the middle way of right action and right human relations.

14

What Is Ascension?

Ascension is the ability to materialize and dematerialize oneself at will, the ability to materialize whatever is needed, or desired instantly. It is a feeling of oneness at all times with God and one's brothers and sisters in Christ. It is a consciousness of being a world server. It is the power to command your life to be as you desire it, by the power of your word or thoughts. It is the ability to bi-locate and achieve physical immortality. Some of the ascended masters have lived in their bodies for thousands of years.

Many people today are looking for the next step leading to ascension, because we are beginning to understand that it is possible to ascend while still in our bodies. Ascension is taking steps to expand your consciousness and be of service to your fellow man. When we love our fellow human unconditionally, we begin to understand that we are all one in the eyes of God. We must look at each other as brother and sister as we all progress on the path toward God. We are all one, connected to each other as human beings, and we must look beyond race, color, or culture. The consciousness of ascension is total unconditional love. Greet everyone with the full recognition and the realization that we are all reflections of God walking on the Earth.

It is important for us to realize that with every word, thought, or deed we have each day, our soul is either ascending or descending. We must control our thoughts, words, and deeds before we can make any true advancement on the way to ascension, which must be accomplished before we can reach the third initiation. There can be some small degrees of imperfection, but we must correct such problems immediately, and ask forgiveness for them. As human beings, none of us are in the perfect state until we reach ascension, which is controlling our energy vibrations by controlling our reactions, emotions, words, thoughts, and deeds. Our emotions are controlled by our minds, but we let them rule us from our lower chakras, which means personal gratification, desires, money, and all the things on Earth we feel we must have to be number one. The materialism of this world is only glamor that holds us captive to the false belief that it is the best way to get what we want now. The only thing that lasts beyond death is the love we have shown to others, and how we have helped, shared, and comforted others. Those who understand the rules of ascension know that being of service to others on Earth is the best way to move further along the path back to God.

Many people chatter away, feeling they are not considered worthy unless they control the conversation. They think they must talk constantly to be noticed, but that is one of the worst things they can do, because they are accountable for every word coming out of their mouth. We usually see this happening when people start talking before they start thinking. Often they are being spiteful, or gossiping about others. When people are insecure about themselves, they act this way to fit in with others. We must correct this way of thinking before we can move toward ascension.

If we consider ascension from an energy perspective, we see that it constantly involves an energy exchange, because everything is made up of energy vibrating at different rates of speed. Positive words and actions vibrate faster than negative words or actions, and they change our energy field. When we notice what we are thinking, we attract to ourselves the positive energies of love, joy, harmony, peace, and more. Like energy will attract more of the same, because this is one of the universal laws.

Ascension is a very natural occurrence that all of us will ultimately achieve, and it is just a matter of time. The idea is to shorten the time needed, reducing the number of future lives on the wheel of rebirth by applying and focusing our energies on spiritual growth in our current life. This will shorten the amount of time we must spend going through the same thing life after life. Our negative ego, or lower chakras, are the ones we have to guard against, because they will try to take us on illusionary and glamorous paths going the wrong direction, taking us further away from God.

We have a very special opportunity to ascend during this time period on the Earth, because we have the help of the ascended masters, Christ, and many other enlightened beings who are here now to help us ascend. Mass ascension has occurred in the past, tied to the evolution of Sanat Kumara, the Planetary Logos of Shamballa. Whenever He reaches another plateau in his cosmic evolution, mass ascension occurs.

When two or more cycles come together, that period is extremely important in Earth's history, and we are now in such a transition time of starting a new cycle. Now we can move ahead extremely fast toward ascension. All the effort we make from now through the next 100 years will be magnified many times over, because of the evolution of Sanat Kumara, which will affect the Earth as well, because His consciousness encompasses the entire planet, and everything on it.

First Initiation

The First Initiation is regarded by the masters as showing how much perseverance and determination we have to be earnestly admitted on the ascension path. It also marks the commencement of the ascended masters as our teachers, as they begin to work with us in our lives. Many times we must abandon the old way of life that no longer serves us. Initiates' live are beginning to be controlled by the Christ Consciousness, which is the consciousness of responsibility, unconditional love, and service.

Second Initiation

The second initiation relates to the control of our words, thoughts, deeds, and the emotional body. This initiation is usually the hardest one for people to pass, and it often takes many lifetimes to complete. Once it is completed, the next one usually follows in the same life or the next one.

Third Initiation

The third initiation is when we must control our emotional body and our self-gratification desires. The keynotes of this initiation are dedication, glamor, and devotion. Dedication results in glamor, which is dissipated by devotion. The emotions are brought under control, the mind assumes an increasing importance, and much greater control of the selfish sensitivity of the lower chakras is attained.

At the third initiation we are developing self-mastery over our thoughts, words, and deeds that control our personalities. This initiation is also referred to as the soul merge, in which we become blended and merged with our higher selves and become soul-infused personalities. Our entire personality becomes flooded with Light from above, and we are no longer controlled by our lower minds or desires. Our personality has very high vibrations at this point.

The third initiation is considered by the masters as the first major initiation, because it is administered by Sanat Kumara, the Planetary Logos, whereas the first two initiations are given by the Great White Brotherhood of Ascended Masters. Our minds are primarily responsive to ideas, intuitions, and impulses coming from the soul, and they are receiving energies from our souls, from our spiritual community, and from the Spiritual Hierarchy. At this point, the accumulation of knowledge is unbelievably rapid, and energies from the higher level become available to us.

The third-degree students have merged with their monad, which is a whole group of souls, thus making the soul group conscious. They begin to receive direct information from their higher selves and guides. The third eye is stimulated in this initiation, and, with Sanat Kumara performing the ceremony, a huge volt of spiritual energy is administered, which is a totally unique energy transmitted by Him. He directs extra-planetary energy from His third-eye center to the head center of the initiate, and from there immediately to the initiate's third-eye center, where it is then directed outward into its destined field of service. It is so high a quality that there is no way the initiate can measure its admission and circulation through the head centers. This energy pours through the students out into the world, even though they remain unconscious of its presence.

The third-eye center is placed between the two eyes to signify that the two-fold direction of life energy of the initiate is out into the world and flows upward toward Source. Energy follows thought, so we realize that our thoughts must be consciously projected outward for the incoming divine energies to produce powerful results in the world, which is the major work of the Hierarchy. As the evolutionary process continues, new and higher energies become available, which is a particular opportunity now, as we all prepare for the reappearance of the Christ.

At the third initiation our main focus is to integrate science, direction, and learning to work more closely with the ascended masters. We work to become a more integral part of the masters' group. As we continue working we learn to absorb, transmute, and distribute energy as the major service. The main objective is right direction, which is the result of right reaction. We can then move into understanding the process of the Hierarchy, and how it relates to our soul. Utilizing integration and direction require that we understand hidden, scientific knowledge. Before and immediately after the third initiation, we work mainly on the mental level, and it becomes our main objective to condition and direct our minds to work with the Hierarchy.

Also after the third initiation, the energy is focused as group, or monadic in nature. Part of the awareness that has been shown to us demonstrates how we are no longer the individual unit we assumed ourselves to be. We are actually a part of a group, the Hierarchy, who has the same goals and ideals in mind, all working together to achieve the will of God.

What Is Ascension?

Fourth Initiation

The fourth initiation is called the renunciation, or crucifixion, of all things of the material world. The initiate is renouncing all things associated with the material world, like money, desires, material things, self-gratification, and lower vibrations. The word crucifixion does not mean death and torture, which does not represent the true meaning of the fourth initiation.

Part of the reason that the fourth initiation is called the renunciation, is because we realize that we have successfully completed a direct line of energy from the Hierarchy. Our soul, which has been the supposed source of our existence, guide, and mentor, is no longer needed. We now have a relation as a soul-infused personality directly connected to the One, and our three-fold spirit is now immortal. Our soul body is relinquished, and it disappears, as it is no longer needed. We feel bereft and are apt to call out — as did the Master Jesus — "My God, my God, why hast Thou forsaken me?" This great act of renunciation marks the moment when we have nothing in us that relates to the three worlds of human evolution. Our contact with those three worlds in the future is purely voluntary for purposes of service.

This renunciation signifies that we are a non-fluctuating and unchanging member of the kingdom of God — the Hierarchy. Our soul consciously renounces all and turns its back upon the material world, finally and forever. We have mastered all the uses of the three worlds of experiment, experience, and expression, and they now stand liberated. We are lifted up by the renunciation, because we have made it out of the world of material possessions, and because we no longer have any interest in them, nor do we feel any hold that material possessions may have ever had over us. The person is completely detached. It is interesting to note that Master Jesus underwent the renunciation (fourth) initiation, while at the same time the Christ Spirit was raised up at the seventh, or resurrection, initiation. So the two stories of these two great disciples are parallel, having both successfully completed their work, moving on to the next step in their journey back toward God.

At the fourth initiation our physical body is totally filled with divine light, and we are referred to as an arhat by the Hierarchy, which means that we are off the wheel of rebirth or reincarnation. We no longer have to experience pain and suffering, because we no longer have a physical body as such. Our body is now of totally restructured matter — immortal and indestructible. We are now considered full-fledged members of the Great White Brotherhood.

At the fourth initiation the person is considered a master of wisdom and lord of compassion. We are no longer souls in prison. We have been lifted out of the lower world and totally liberated. We have become an unchanging, permanent member of the spiritual Hierarchy, the Great White Brotherhood. From this point on, we are guided by intuition, pure reason, and complete knowledge, illuminated by love. The fifth initiation usually follows closely upon the fourth initiation. All knowledge, science, wisdom, and experience gathered in past lives are now in our possession.

The Fifth Initiation

The fifth initiation is also known as the resurrection or ascension, because we realize we are free and no longer on the wheel of rebirth. We are liberated, and we are now ready for a new world of experiences. As a master of wisdom, we realize that we no longer need a physical body. Our body is now a body of light, which has its own type of substance.

At this point in the ascension process we determine what kind of body we want, and what it will look like. We can build a body with which to approach incoming students and those who have not taken the higher initiations. Most of the masters working with humans preserve the body in which they took the fifth initiation, instead of manifesting a new body. Djwhal Khul was a fifth-degree initiate while writing most of the Alice Bailey books, and when he ascended in that lifetime, he preserved that body. Kuthumi, Djwhal Khul's teacher, chose to build a new one.

Today many people have taken one or another of these initiations. There are some great master teachers working in the physical world as servers to humanity under the Hierarchy, and there will be many more in the next 100 years. Some do not know their true Hierarchical status, since they were made to forget at birth in order to do certain work. Information about Hierarchical status is for those who work with the Hierarchy but do not remember consciously why it is so important to them at this time to be of service to humanity or to learn more about the ascended masters.

There are a total of nine initiations, and most people are now taking the first three; the fourth is the half-way point. The fifth initiation is a huge change for us, as it takes us into the realms of cosmic ascension, which opens up a whole new vista of possibilities. The final two initiations are extra-planetary, and consist of vast proportions of consciousness out into the cosmos.

15
Purifying Yourself for Ascension

You may have felt time speeding up, which in turn is causing the evolution of our planet to speed up at the same rate. As evolution speeds up, we must be ready to be called upon to help our fellow humans. The ascended masters are looking for people who are applying themselves in their current situation, to find qualified applicants to help them serve humanity. They feel people by their vibrations, and they can identify those who, with a certain amount of training, would fill their needs.

People are now acting out of their emotional bodies, which is the focal point of their personality. They are ruled by their emotions, which must be shifted to the mental level. Since evolution has sped up, certain things have to be brought about before people can qualify to be used as reliable workers, true as tempered steel, for the purpose of helping our race.

The first step to raising our vibration is to purify our physical body, which is needed because it is much harder for those with dense bodies to contact high vibration. It is impossible for higher knowledge and guidance to be transmitted through a dense body. In the same manner, it is impossible for the higher currents of thought to be received by the lowly evolved brain. So the refinement of our physical bodies is essential.

Our physical body can become purified by eating healthy, wholesome food. The best way is a vegetarian diet, chosen with careful discrimination. A good diet requires eating only those vegetables and fruits that vitalize and energize the body. Careful judgment must be shown in our choice of food, including the size of the portions at each meal. Healthy organic food served in small portions that is perfectly prepared is all that is required for the body. All that is needed to keep our body vitalized is milk, honey, whole-wheat bread, oranges (very important), bananas, raisins, nuts, some potatoes, rice, and all the vegetables that contact the sun. Sunshine is needed daily. Avoid the sun from 11 a.m. until 2 p.m., when the rays are too intense, but be out in the sun daily for at least 30 minutes, which gives the body vitamin D, and is necessary for our health. If you cannot be in the sun daily, then take vitamin D in pill form along with a good multiple vitamin and mineral once daily.

It is important to be clean on the inner and outer levels. In addition, you should sleep seven to eight hours a night. When you follow this regimen over a period of time your whole physical body shifts gradually, until ultimately you have a body composed of higher vibrations.

Other things that can facilitate purification are certain sounds and music that stimulate higher vibrations. Certain types of music that impede the vibrations of the electromagnetic field of our body can be stressful and harmful to our system. It is best to listen to music that is soothing, harmonic, and beautiful, like classical music. Certain colors will stimulate our vibrational system as well. Using the violet-colored lights will help us cleanse our auric fields and remove energy that is not beneficial to us.

Being of service means that we cannot fail to carry out our mission because of a physical liability, or lack of sufficient rest. We must take care of our physical body with good healthy food, plenty of rest, and adequate sleep. We typically eat four times what we need, as a general rule. When we desire to be of service, we keep ourselves ready to be called into action at any time.

Take a little time each day to still your emotional body. It should become still and clear as a mirror, so that it may reflect perfectly. Your aim should be to control your emotions, and not let them control you. Most people live according to the wants and desires of their emotional body. Our consciousness must be raised to the mental level, so the emotional body does not dictate what we do, or how we live. We must not let the emotional body control our thoughts, or raise the tides of desire. We must keep it still, serene, unruffled, quiet, at rest, and clear, like a mirror. When we let our emotions rule us, we are not in a space to accurately transmit the wishes, the desires, and the aspirations of our higher self.

We must constantly watch all our desires, motives and wishes that cross our personal horizon daily, emphasizing those that are of a high order and forcing out those on negative levels, which will help us to react differently and change our awareness of the situation.

We should make a daily attempt to contact our higher self and to reflect its wishes in our life. At first you might make mistakes, but little by little the building process moves forward, and your emotional body gradually shifts upward until your thoughts are on much higher levels.

Stilling the emotional body each day for a period of time will help quiet your mind. It is best to begin with quieting the emotions and let this lead up to quieting the mind, which will be of great assistance in meditating for longer periods.

You must discover for yourself what emotions — like love, fear, worry, desire, discouragement, or even over-sensitivity to opinions — cause you to have violent reactions. Then you must learn to overcome the emotion by immediately changing your negative reaction to positive thoughts, and not allowing it to rule your emotions.

On our mental level we seek to build information and to gather knowledge and facts. We need to train scientifically on an intellectual basis, so that as time goes on it remains a stable foundation for divine wisdom. Wisdom supersedes knowledge, yet it requires knowledge as the first step. You pass through the Hall of Learning before entering the Hall of Wisdom. To train your mind, you acquire a steady accumulation of knowledge and achieve control of your emotional body so your higher self can dominate, which allows your creative mind of your higher self to lead you to higher inspiration.

Purifying Yourself for Ascension

When you show control in all areas of your life, it will affect the three departments of physical, emotional, and mental well being. We seek perfection in action, in our life, and in the details of our environment. Life progresses by small steps, and when each step is taken at the right time, each moment will be occupied wisely, leading to a long distance being covered and a life well spent. The ascended masters watch all on Earth to see how they are handling these details in everyday life. They look for those who can handle these details with faithful action and love. The people they are looking for can be depended on to move into greater responsibility. How can they depend upon someone, who, in everyday matters, does sloppy work and can't handle an emergency or crisis?

The ascended masters are on call at night to help you while you sleep, if you call on them before you go to sleep, asking for their help. You can also call on them to help you move toward initiations, which are like classrooms of learning and are marked by certain tests at night to show how you are progressing.

The first initiation basically shows the masters how much determination and interest you show in the Great White Brotherhood, which lets the master teachers know you are ready to move forward in learning and work with them on the higher levels. Things begin to get harder and more involved at the second initiation, which marks your control of your emotional body. Controlling your emotional body is very difficult to accomplish, and no excess emotion is permitted, though strong feelings of love are allowed. Love is the law of the system; it is constructive and stabilizing. No fear, worry or care should be allowed to shake your emotional body at all. You practice serenity, stability, and a sense of dependence on God's law. A joyous confidence should be your usual attitude. You harbor no jealousy, no cloudy grey depression, no greed, nor self-pity. You realize that all people are brothers and sisters as one, and you go calmly on your way.

Each initiation is made up of four smaller initiations, stages of learning within each level that show our progress as each one is completed. These initiations are on the emotional level and are called the initiations of earth, fire, water, and air. They culminate in your second initiation.

Your goal should be to have a life of service to humanity, to raise your vibrations to qualify to be of help to the ascended masters on Earth. When you gain knowledge and it is not passed on and shared with wise discrimination, it causes stagnation, obstruction, and pain. Food absorbed by the human body, if not digested and passed through the system, causes these same conditions. The new age has much to teach, and it should be shared with those in the world who are ready to hear about it, and not kept for your exclusive use.

When you are ready to be of service, three things are most important — your motive, your method, and your attitude following action. To your utmost ability, you should do the master's will and perform the work to be done by you in co-operation with God's plan. Then, once having done your part, you are not to be concerned with the result of the action you are instructed to carry out, because you can't see the whole plan of the ascended masters. Leave the details to the masters who are guiding the human race to work everything out, and know that they understand far more than we can as human beings.

What You Can Do

You can use hypnotherapy to help clear out blockages on the soul level that can keep you from advancing in this life. Your soul is immortal, and you have had many past lives that may have an effect on the way you are living today. You carry things forward on a soul level that have affected you in past lives, usually in a very traumatic way. These past traumas may have been the cause of a death in a past life, which could come out now as a fear or phobia. These phobias can be healed via past-life regression.

A light trance state is when you are doing something like driving, and your mind is not fully focused on what you are doing all the time. For instance, at some time you might have found yourself driving past your exit, because your mind had drifted onto other thoughts. Since you had already learned to drive, your driving skills are stored in your subconscious mind, which does not have to be fully engaged all the time to drive or to do other activities you have learned. When you are engaged in these mundane activities, your conscious mind can drift off in other directions. This is a light trance state, because it is so subtle that we do not associate it as a shift from the conscious mind to the subconscious.

Being in a trance state generally makes us receptive to hypnotic suggestion, so you will be likely to experience relaxation, sleepiness, a rigidity or limpness in the muscles of your arms and legs, a feeling of cold or warmth, or a tingling sensation. These are just some of the ways you might experience hypnosis. Being in a trance is a very natural experience of a different level of the mind, and you are always in control. Your experience is assisted by your hypnotherapist, but you are the one in control at all times.

You cannot be made to do anything you think is unacceptable, or which would violate your values or accepted patterns of behavior. It is important to remember that you can terminate the trance state at any time. If you choose to enter the trance state, you can also choose to leave it at any time. It is not possible to be left in a trance state by the hypnotherapist, for you would either return to full consciousness on your own or enter a natural sleep and awaken after a pleasant nap. No one has ever disappeared or been unable to return from a trance state. Those silly examples of hypnosis on television, which are not really the way it all works, have instead caused the public to fear hypnosis when they really don't even know what it is, or how it works. The truth is, it is so effective that it is being used by the government in many ways.

Our subconscious remembers everything we have ever experienced in this life, as well as our past lives. We can access the subconscious mind through hypnosis, and we can use it as a tool to improve our lives in many ways. Hypnosis can help us fight pain, quit smoking, heal phobias or fear, reduce stress, lose weight, increase motivation, and improve athletic performance, which are just some of the many ways that hypnosis is being used today.

16

Regeneration of the Body

Our endocrine system is the key to working with the etheric body, the web system, and the physical body. We must address all three parts of our physical body and bring them together in a harmonious healthy way of life.

After we reach adulthood and begin to move into middle age, our thyroid begins to play a bigger part in regulating our aging process. It can be stimulated to delay aging by controlling the metabolism process.

The Thyroid

The thyroid secretes and distributes the antitoxin that reverses the body's aging and keeps it youthful and vibrant. It gets especially activated when you raise your vibration, and the entire endocrine system becomes involved.

One method of rejuvenating the thyroid after 45 is to eat vitamin-producing foods. The vitamins activate and increase the hormones within the body. They act on the physical level rather than the chemical level, because they are enzymes and, therefore catalyzers.

Our emotions also affect the thyroid secretions and must be controlled. If fear is overcome completely, the thyroid will be undisturbed by any negative emotions. Love overcomes fear completely and stimulates the action of the thyroid gland immediately. When your thyroid is brought to a certain vibration where spiritual perception takes place, your rejuvenation becomes active and permanent. Your thyroid actually reverses your aging process and your body starts getting more youthful. The changes are permanent and can be accomplished in a very short time.

Your Breath

The breath can be utilized to take more and more oxygen into your body to help stimulate your thyroid in relation to the respiration of your body and cause it to produce more thyroxin, which plays an important part in oxidizing the material that is thrown off and also in bringing the oxygen into a condition through which your body can use it, putting it into your bloodstream as well. It has been proven that bringing more oxygen into your body can help prevent cancer and other fatal diseases. Using your breath to bring more Prana (oxygen) into your body raises its vibration on all levels. The great athletes are aware of their breath and how to control it. They know that their breathing has to be coordinated so they can control their body and mind and be in tune with all their actions. Each cell in our body requires oxygen to maintain its life, and cells that are deprived of oxygen die.

Many people who suffer from illnesses like depression and fatigue are unaware of their breathing, even to the extent that they hardly breathe at all. They use only the upper part of their lungs to exchange air, which is just barely enough air to allow them to survive, this is called shallow breathing. Most people breathe this way, especially women who are taught not to push out their abdomen. In order to fill the lungs to full capacity, breathing must be done from the abdomen; the belly-button moves upward toward the lungs. When it is done correctly, breathing this way completely fills your lungs without any effort on your part. We actually live in an oxygen-starved society today.

When God created humankind, breath was essential to being a living human being. All of the great religions have been aware of how important breath is, and they incorporate breathing techniques into their physical disciplines.

It is a good idea to become aware of your breath several times a day and to do conscious breathing. If you don't know if you are doing shallow breathing, you can lie flat on the floor on your back and put your hand over your belly button. If you are pulling this area upward when you breathe, then you are breathing deeply enough, if you do not detect any movement or very little, then you are not breathing enough to fill your lungs to capacity. It would be a good idea to check your breathing several times a day to make sure it is coming from your abdomen. Practice this process until you know how it feels when your body is getting enough oxygen.

A great way to reduce stress during the day is to practice conscious breathing until you feel your body making a shift to a higher-energy level. When we don't breathe deeply enough, we are depriving our brain and our nervous and muscular systems, as well as the rest of the body, from receiving the oxygen they need.

Practice conscious breathing as often as possible. For short periods of time, breathe in joy and love, and breathe out fear or whatever you want to release. You can change this to suit whatever your needs are; for instance, breathe in good things, and, on the exhalation of your breath, send out all the negative things that are no longer for your highest good.

This practice will change your entire auric field, and anyone looking at your energy field will be able to see the difference right away.

Prana

Prana is the vital energy of the universe. The word Akasha means space, and the whole universe was projected out of Akasha through the energy of Prana. Akasha is the infinite, all-pervading energy of the universe, and Prana is the infinite, all-pervading energy of the universe we call cosmic energy. All the forms of our universe are sustained by it.

Patanjali, the sage who codified yoga science around 200 B.C., explains that the control of Prana is the regulation of inhalation and exhalation, which is accomplished by eliminating the pause between inhalation and exhalation, or by expanding the pause through retention. Therefore, by regulating the motion of the lungs, the heart and the vagus nerve are controlled.

REGENERATION OF THE BODY

The human body is sustained by the same Prana or energy that sustains the universe, and it is through the manifestation of Prana that all body functions are possible and coordinated.

In the Eastern teachings, the Sanskrit word, Pranayama is the study of the breath. One who has learned to control Prana has learned to control all the physical and mental energies of the universe. The person has also learned to control his/her body and mind. All yogic breathing exercises — advanced or basic — enable the students to control their minds by understanding Prana.

Prana is the actual life within the oxygen. It is what gives force to electricity and gives consciousness to mind. In other words, it is the reality existing within, standing back of, and sustaining all the lesser forces. It is called the Spirit of God in the Scriptures. Prana is one of the elements of Spirit, as spirit is not only energy but also intelligence, substance or matter.

The mind stands like a dividing line between us and reality. When you come in touch with Prana, you can learn to control your mind, for it is tightly fastened to Prana as a kite is to a string. When the string is held skillfully, the kite, which wants to fly here and there, is controlled and flies in the direction desired.

Prana energy is subtle in form, and its most external manifestation is your breath. It is through the control of respiration that the yogi can manipulate the other subtle energies of Prana, which may explain the use of the same word for the universal energy, as well as for the specific Prana-governing respiration. The importance of this specific Prana in allowing us access to the subtler energies of the cosmic Prana can also be seen in the fact that death results when we stop breathing.

The autonomic nervous system regulates processes in your body that are not normally under your voluntary control, such as secretion by the digestive organs, the beating of your heart, and the movement of your lungs. The study of your breath is thus intimately connected with the autonomic nervous system and brings its functions under your conscious control through the functioning of your lungs. The act of respiration is for the most part involuntary, but voluntary control in this area is easily achieved, for you can control and modulate the depth, duration, and frequency of your breath quite readily. It is for this reason that control of the breath constitutes an obvious starting point toward attainment of control over the functioning of your autonomic nervous system.

Controlling your breath and calming your nerves is prerequisite to controlling the mind, and having control of your mind is prerequisite to the ultimate subjugation of the universal energy of Prana. To the yogi, body, breath, nerves, mind, Prana, and the universe are all part of one whole, and there is no distinction between them.

Study of these systems will show how they are all interrelated and how they work with each other. This information seems to indicate that the Eastern teachings discovered the inner working of the human body thousands of years ago. On the other hand, while modern medicine has brought many advances, it is only beginning to understand these intricate workings of the body, and how they are all interrelated. It is slow to give up its mechanistic view of the body. Western civilization is just beginning to understand how advanced some of the ancient civilizations were, and what they were able to accomplish.

To most people in the west, including the Americas, the study of the breath in the teachings of the mystics has not been included as a prerequisite to the spiritual path. The Native Americans did not concentrate on the breath as the key to raising vibrations, or spiritual awareness. They mostly based their beliefs on the oneness of all things, such as Mother Earth, all nature, including animals, the stars, the cosmos, and every living thing, thereby merging their awareness into the oneness of all things.

Most Americans never consider their breathing, but it is now important to become more aware of this part of ourselves in order to promote good health and spiritual growth. There are many avenues of spiritual growth available to us, but to speed up this process, we must be aware that breath plays a key role. Our breath must be part of our ascension process if we are interested in rapidly expanding our spiritual awareness.

We have always been taught that attention is the secret to success when dealing with spiritual forces. Deep, sincere, abiding attention to the surrounding spiritual forces and complete openness of mind are the necessary attitudes to have in order to recognize our inner breath. The key is to be conscious of our breath, letting ourselves expand into the ethers and then pulling the interpenetrating life force (Prana), or spiritual ethers down, until they are drawn within our whole being.

It is not the mere act of breathing that draws this cosmic life force into the body. Unless we give definite attention to our physical breathing, it is not definitely engaged. It is a life force, which is so much finer than our physical air that it is not affected by mere physical processes.

When we practice breathing from the abdomen it is important that we cultivate the habit of harmonious, rhythmic breathing along with pulling the air up from the abdomen. Breathing between 16 and 20 breaths per minute is considered average, but when both inhalation and exhalation become slower and smoother, breathing becomes easy. Scientists have discovered that during inhalation the capillaries are also filled with enough oxygen, so lengthening the inhalation increases the time available for this transfer to take place. Rhythmic breathing from the diaphragm also brings more air and oxygen into your lungs' air sacs and into the bloodstream. It increases the return of oxygen-depleted blood to your lungs, and sends an increased blood supply to your capillaries.

Rhythmic breathing exercises should be practiced on a regular basis. Exhalation should be through the nostrils, and there should be no sound in the breath. After exhaling completely, inhalation begins again, and minimize the pause, then again breathe through the nostrils, making no sound. Continue with this rhythmic breathing filling the lungs completely with each breath.

To increase your spiritual growth, it is a good idea to practice rhythmic breathing exercises 10 times a day for at least two months, with gradual and equal prolongation of both inhalation and exhalation. The body will experience a sense of deep relaxation and rest, which will also help reduce your stress and depression.

When practicing these breathing techniques it is a good idea for every phase of your mind to be free, and your body completely relaxed. You will have a sense of complete freedom, and total expansion, as if the cells of your body were actually moving out from each other until they stand apart. This practice may be continued until your forget your sense of physical limitation altogether, until you are in the most perfect state to bring Prana of a high level into your whole being. Using visualization and employing all your senses to see, feel, and know that the desired results are happening in your body will help to make them all manifest, as well as help keep your body young and vibrant.

Practicing full rhythmic breathing not only vitalizes the body, but it also enlivens the mind. The reason we do not think clearly is because the mind is too tense and compressed to function freely. Full breathing allows the mind to recall memories without effort, and anything you want to remember or know comes easily into your mind.

What we know as energy and substance are but two aspects of a single primal energy — Prana, or Spirit. We may truly say that Prana is one of the elements of Spirit, for Spirit is not only energy, but also intelligence and substance. It is more subtle than ether. The western world defines ether as Prana, though there is a difference in the subtlety and the activity of the two. Ether is nascent, while Prana is always active. Ether is Prana becoming, or coming out, toward manifestation. All of the finer forces of nature are divisions and media through which Prana works.

When the human body dies or any material form disintegrates, it goes back into Prana — first into the various forms of energy, and then back into Universal and primal force. If Prana were constantly received into our whole being, our flesh would be eternally quickened and would become more and more animated and alive, and the last enemy would be overcome. There are those who overcome old age and death with or through an understanding of Prana. They rebuild the body with the Pranic influence. This happens in a slight degree every time one sleeps or rests. When you add conscious attention to the Pranic presence by completely relaxing your mind and body, your attention breathes the ever-present Prana into and through your whole being, which assures that you attain the greatest degree of renewal of your mind and body.

The primal attribute of being is intelligence, and Prana is the activity of consciousness, or vital force of creation, and substance is the form through which both act. Intelligence, life, and substance are the trinity of elements in the first cause, as defined by the western world.

Prana embraces both the substance and life elements — the vehicles or media through which intelligence moves to direct and determine the created forms. This primal intelligence, life, and substance are God Almighty in action, but they must become a conscious fact in you. You select it to be of conscious use to you.

17

Etheric Body & Chakra System

The etheric body is the energy form that controls, governs and conditions your outer physical body. Your etheric body cannot be seen with your human eyes, because it is very subtle and is made up of a very fine mesh of interlocking and circulating lines of energy that are connected with the energy flowing from the higher levels of the planetary center. This energy is then transmitted from the Hierarchy to humanity from the Planetary Logos at Shamballa — Sanat Kumara. Additionally, these lines of energy and this closely interlocking system are related to the seven chakra centers in your etheric energy body. Each chakra corresponds to a certain type of this incoming Pranic energy, which is constantly flowing throughout the solar system and the entire universe. The etheric body is subject to constant change due to this energy flowing through it.

Your physical body is made up of three parts — your etheric body, your web network of fine tubes that transmit energy throughout your body, and your dense physical body. Your etheric body extends outside the physical body by a few inches to as much as several feet or more and penetrates every single part of the physical body. It is regulated through your chakra system before your physical body can use it properly. Your etheric body is where disease appears first, and then it moves into the physical cellular level. When your chakras are blocked or out of balance in some way, it can create illness in the physical body.

Your etheric body is finely textured, like gossamer strands, and it creates a network with millions of tiny energy lines that the Eastern teachings call "nadis." These nadis are the carriers of energy, and the type of energy they carry at a particular time depends upon your level of consciousness then. Their energy affects your physical body when a responsive chakra center perceives its corresponding energy and is stimulated, which affects the nerves in the immediate area. The seven chakras are not within your physical body, but rather they exist in etheric matter in your auric field around your body.

The endocrine glands are closely associated with your etheric chakras. These master glands regulate your physical body in many ways. Medicine now understands that the endocrine system is especially related to motivation, emotion, and feelings. It is a very complex system that is attuned to, and regulates the endocrine glands. Seven endocrine glands in your physical body correspond to your seven chakras:

o The sexual glands are associated with the base chakra.
o The reproduction cells correspond to the second chakra.
o The adrenal glands are located on top of the kidneys and relate to the third chakra.
o The thymus gland resides beside the heart and is attached to the fourth chakra.
o The thyroid and parathyroid are located in the neck and relate to the fifth chakra.
o The pineal gland is located in the brain and attaches to the sixth chakra.
o The pituitary gland lies on top of the spine and connects to the seventh chakra.

The three highest glands of the endocrine system are the thyroid, pineal, and the pituitary, each of which is not composed of the endocrine gland alone. Instead, it is associated with a nerve center, the solar plexus, and an organ. The pituitary gland is associated with a neural complex called the hypothalamus that is a very special control center in the body. Both the pituitary and the hypothalamus are endocrine and neural centers.

Five of the chakra centers are found in the etheric spinal column. Energy passes through the vertebrae of the spine, and circulates throughout the etheric body, then into the actual physical body. Physically the crown chakra is located just above the top of your head, another is just in front of your eyes and forehead, and the third is at the back of your head, just above where the spinal column ends. This makes eight chakras, but are only seven, because the center at the back of the head is not counted in the initiation process, any more than is the spleen.

The impact of these energies upon the etheric body is very potent. responding in our physical body through our seven major sets of endocrine glands. The energy of our blood is activated when it moves through these endocrine glands. The Bible says, "The blood is life."

The incoming energy has created an outlet through the blood via the glands, and through the nervous system via the millions of energy lines or nadis. Two aspects of energy can be transmitted by these systems, depending upon the person. If you are coming from your lower carnal mind, your energy can be on that level, or if you are coming from a higher spiritual level of thoughts, it can be on the higher levels of divine love. Your free will determines how you will use this energy, which is available to all.

In order to understand the etheric body and energy as a general rule, you must understand that there is no possible separation anywhere, even beyond our planetary life. The concept of separateness is an illusion of the human mind. Everything — every form all the way down to the individual cell — is intimately related to each other through Earth's etheric body — the furniture in your house, the flowers, all the animals, and all people are sharing with you the vast energy fields that constantly circulate through every person, place, or thing. There is only One Life, pouring through the mass of forms of energy which make up our planet. We are all one! All things exist within this planetary etheric energy body so that a cohesive, coherent, expressive whole is presented to our physical eyes, which is not the whole picture, but most people only believe what they can see.

ETHERIC BODY & CHAKRA SYSTEM

To the great teachers, or Hierarchy, of the planet, this energy is seen as one great unfolding consciousness. Lines of light pass from form to form. Some are bright and some are dim; some move or circulate quickly, others are slow. This energy moves throughout all things, and comes from different directions. All these energies are in a constant circulating movement all the time. There is not one single cell in the body that is not touched by this living, moving energy. There is not a single form that is left out of this inflow and outflow. This energy is in touch with all things, and is in complete touch with the Divine intention of the three major planetary centers of Shamballa, the Hierarchy, and Humanity. The Will of God is known at Shamballa, and the members of the Hierarchy work to carry out the Will of God through Humanity.

The etheric body chakras are the crossing points of energies which make up seven triangles or transformed points. From the angle of Shamballa, the centers in a human resemble a triangle with a point at the center.

"Energy follows thought," so if you are focused in your solar-plexus chakra, the energy can be lifted up to a higher chakra by using fixed and determined thought, which serves a higher purpose — the lower chakras below the diaphragm will atrophy from disuse. When we raise these energies up to the higher chakras, it produces the needed changes that raise our vibration and help us evolve.

By learning and sharing this information about the etheric body and the chakra system, we can help others, because these energies can be stimulated or vitalized as needed to help others evolve, or to help them heal their bodies. People of a destructive nature can be helped to rid themselves of unwanted entities or energies, thereby aiding their mental, physical, and spiritual well-being.

The etheric body and all of its many manifestations is accepted by many scientific schools who study energy, which is now regarded as all that is, and manifestation is seen as the shape of forms within the sea of energies. Other energy is where those forms live and move and have their being, and still others are in process of animating both the forms and all connected with them. Forms exist within forms, so when you sit in your room, you are a form within a form. The room you are in is itself a form within a house, and that house (another form) is probably one of many similar houses, placed side by side, which together are composing a still larger form of a neighborhood. All these diverse forms are composed of substance coordinated and brought together by some thinker who created a material form. All these buildings are composed of living energies, vibrating in relation to the other, yet owning their own quality and their own qualified life.

The entire universe is etheric and vital in nature — extending beyond the grasp of the greatest mind of the age. The cosmic etheric area is the field of untold energies and the basis of all astrological computations. It is the playground of all historical cycles — cosmic, systemic, and planetary. It is related to the constellations, the worlds of suns, the most distant stars, the many planets, our own solar system, and to this planet where we live and have our being, which includes the smallest forms of life known to science.

As we raise our vibrations, our physical body activates our chakra system to a higher level. We raise our energy up from our lower chakras to our three higher ones, which are our heart, throat, and head. This process begins as we start cleansing and purifying our physical bodies along with our spiritual development. When our chakra system processes Prana correctly, all our physical organs become vitalized, which protects us from disease and common body ailments. Western medical doctors should be doing much more preventive care than they are today, which can be accomplished by studying the etheric body's chakra system. Most doctors today still only view the body as a machine and treat the symptom, without identifying the root cause of the disease.

When the vibrations in our body rise, our energy is slowly brought up from our lower chakra centers to our three higher centers in the body

ETHERIC BODY & CHAKRA SYSTEM

of our heart, throat, and head. Once the Kundalini fire begins to rise, it blends with other energies in the spinal column and reaches a center between the lower part of the shoulder blades, which is the point of conjunction and complete merging, which is when the first initiation allows the Prana to come in with greatly increased velocity.

After the merging takes place, the chakra system becomes a fourth-dimensional action center, like wheels turning upon themselves. As the fire of Kundalini and Prana proceed with their work, and you become more and more cleared, your centers become more active, and the flame of spirit comes downwards to create a flame of brilliance that issues from the top of your head. This flame spreads throughout the body's chakra system, creating a united flame of light that makes the chakras look as if they are one. We can see this brilliant light when we gaze upon those who have succeeded in obtaining this level.

The merging and blending of Prana in the chakra system destroys the etheric web, after which we can receive the fire of Spirit more abundantly. The first three initiations allow this process to be perfected, which leads to the fourth initiation, where all barriers are completely burned away. We must consciously bring about our own liberation, because these results are self-induced, and once we do, we become an ascended master — one who has broken the wheel of rebirth and no longer has to die and be reborn to work out karma from past lives.

If you try to manipulate this process too quickly without the purification of your body that is required, you stand may be in danger of possession, insanity, physical death, or dire disease in some part of the body. Another possibility that could occur is that your sex impulse could become amplified, because the body is not pure enough to withstand the uniting of the flames, because the chakra system has not been sufficiently cleansed and purified to carry the Prana. A channel up the spine that is still clogged and blocked acts as a barrier that will return the energy to the lower chakras, thus lowering the body's vibration, attracting undesirable energy and entities that will destroy, tear, and ruin what is left of your etheric body.

Your etheric body must be directed solely by the Light of the Spirit, who works through love, and is love. We must seek this unification and merging because we seek liberation and purification in order to form a higher union with Spirit, not because we desire material gratification. This union must not be desired for selfish ends, but rather for the goal and scope of working in groups for greater service to the human race.

Humanity should realize how important it is to understand the source of energy or Prana that comes to us from the cosmos. We receive this Prana first through a major center between our shoulder blades, from which it flows into the etheric spinal column, then out into the etheric body, and finally into the actual physical body by way of the three major centers that are between our shoulder blades, above our diaphragm, and our spleen.

In order to develop our etheric body, the major centers of the body need to be exposed to the rays of the sun, which will help improve our physical vitality and health. The three centers form a radiant etheric triangle in the body. The etheric network of fine channels disseminates the Pranic energy throughout the entire system of the body into every cell. The vital essence from the sun passes into the etheric spleen, where it is intensified or devitalized, according to the condition of that organ. If you are healthy, the energy you receive will be augmented by your own individual vibration and will be boosted up before it is passed into the physical spleen. If you are in a poor health, the energy will be slowed down and lowered.

Each chakra should be visualized as a whirling vortex of energy passing from each chakra to the next, forming an almost separate circulatory system. This vital Pranic fluid circulates three times through and between the three main centers before it finally passes out from them into the system's periphery. This final circulation carries the Prana by way of the fine interlacing channels to every part of the body, which becomes entirely saturated by these energies. The Prana, including any particular human quality that was added to it during its circulation through the auric field, is then expelled from the entire system on the opposite side of the spleen from where it entered.

The solar system receives Prana from cosmic sources via its three centers — Sirius, the Pleiades, and Arcturus — and then redistributes it to all parts of its extended influence, or to the bounds of the solar etheric web. This energy is under the control of the Solar Logos (Helios—our Sun). Earth receives Prana from the solar center and redistributes it via the three receiving centers to all parts of its sphere of influence. This energy is controlled by and, therefore, colored by, the emanations of the Planetary Logos when it passes through the Earth, after which, it has the qualities of the planetary etheric vehicle, and the planetary quality.

Prana varies in vibration and quality according to the entity receiving it. People pass the Prana through their etheric vehicles, color it with their own particular qualities, and so transmit it to the lesser lives that make up their little systems. Thus, the great interaction goes on. All parts blend, merge and are interdependent; and all parts receive, color, qualify and transmit. An endless circulation of Prana goes on with no conceivable beginning or end, but limitation and termination result as the effects of imperfection give way to gradual perfection. Every cycle originates from another cycle and will give way to an ever-higher spiral of perfection. Thus, we have periods of apparent relative perfection leading to periods of even greater perfection.

For our current cycle, our aim is to blend and merge with the fires of mind and spirit until they become one and bring about liberation from our physical bodies into higher realms. The Pranic vehicle is working on three levels, the human, planetary and solar, and the union of these three will be accomplished.

Studying the chakra system and the etheric body facilitates the free movement of this Pranic energy, because when we receive it, we boost our vibration to a higher level and prevent it from being lowered by our body's condition, which is why it is very important to build a purer, more refined physical body, to better receive Prana with less resistance to the rise of Kundalini energy at the appointed time. When we have bodies that are in poor shape, the energy is more disrupted, and our bodies cannot withstand the higher vibrations required for ascension, so when we encounter such higher-vibrating energies, our bodies cannot withstand the necessary purification by fire. Therefore, the more we do to raise our vibrations, the better it will help us adjust to the higher energies when the time comes.

There are many new ways of working with the etheric body and chakra system that have become well known since the 1980s. One of the easiest ways for beginners to start using this energy is to practice what has been called "the laying on of hands," used by Jesus in the Bible. In ancient times it was also called the "King's Touch," and today it is sometimes called "therapeutic touch," or "Reiki."

Reiki Practice

We have a chakra in each hand that makes them more sensitive to energy imbalances in the body, and they can also be used to project energy vibrations to help restore balance in others. We can learn to use our hands as tools for healing, and we all can develop these tools further.

When Jesus used these techniques in the Bible to heal others, He would ask the person if they believed that He could heal them. When they answered "Yes," He said, "your faith has made you whole." These words indicate it was the person's own belief that had actually brought about the healing. It is time we recognize this truth and break out of our limiting belief system. When a person does not believe a healing is possible, it can actually stop the healing from taking place.

It takes practice and persistence to begin to sense these subtle energies. As we continue to use our hands to sense the subtle energies around our bodies, we begin to grow in our awareness. It is a good idea to practice this awareness on a partner, to get objective feedback. Use relaxed concentration; the more relaxed you are, the easier it is to sense the energy and the more sensitive you will become to the subtle energies you are working with. A good way to relax yourself is to close your eyes, breathe deeply and focus on each part of your body individually, starting at your feet and working your way to the top of your head. Mentally send warm, relaxing feelings into each area of the body that you focus on. See the energy, feel it, and imagine it moving.

When you are relaxed, you will experience outside energies more intensely. A phone ringing will seem louder, smells will seem stronger, and light and colors will appear brighter. Touch becomes more sensitive, which then assists us in perceiving and directing energies with our hands more effectively.

Rub the palms of your hands together briskly for about 15 to 30 seconds. Your hands are strong points of sensitivity, and rubbing helps stimulate the chakras in each hand, increasing their overall sensitivity.

Energy follows thought, so wherever your thoughts are focused, so are your energy patterns. Your energy adjusts itself in accordance with your thoughts. For instance, when you tell yourself that you get two colds every winter, your body's systems begin to work and adjust so that we are more susceptible to catching two colds.

We are exposed to many different energies from those around us. Others' thoughts and emotions affect our energy field. Exposure to outside energies can impinge upon our energy field and affect our overall balance. These energies can be anger, fear, and other negative emotions, or they can be energies of warmth and friendship, or those of manipulation. The more aware and sensitive we become to our energy fields, the more we can recognize and control what is allowed to affect them.

Recognizing Energies

An exercise you can do to increase your awareness of how outside energies can impact you is to take a few minutes to relax in a comfortable seated position. You can either close your eyes or keep them open, as you prefer. Hold one hand palm upward, and point the index finger of your other hand into the palm of the first. The finger should be three to six inches away from the other hand. Take slow, deep breaths and as you breathe in and out, imagine the energy building and accumulating in the hand with the pointed index finger. After several minutes of this, slowly begin to rotate your index finger in a small circle. Visualize a stream of energy spiraling out from the index finger to create a circle of energy that touches the palm of the open hand. Don't worry about whether you are imagining it or not, as we are working to prove that energy follows thought.

Pay attention to what you feel within the palm of the hand. Just as in Reiki, the feeling may vary from person to person. You may feel a circle of warmth forming, or it may feel like a thickness, pressure, or tingling in the form of a small circle within the palm of the hand. Sometimes closing your eyes at this point can help you feel the sensations more strongly. The more you project and focus the energy with your mind, the stronger the sensation will become.

Having worked with the palm of the hand, next perform this upon a naked forearm. Visualize and send the energy out through the finger in spirals of energy to impact the forearm. Pay attention to what you feel. With time and practice the kind of sensation you experience will remain much the same, but its intensity will increase.

Another way you can practice is with a partner. First have him or her stand with his/her back to you. Hold your hands about six to 12 inches from your partner's back, palm open and facing the back.

Begin slow, rhythmic breathing. As you breathe in, feel Pranic energy being drawn through your body and into the hands. As you breathe out, visualize and imagine the energy pouring through your hands to your partner's back. Slowly move your hands in a simple geometric pattern — a circle, a square, a triangle, *etc*. Draw this energy pattern on your partner's back with the energy you are directing through your hands. Know in your mind that your partner is feeling it.

Concentrate as you project your energies. Sometimes, if you visualize the stream of energy as a warm red light, it will help your partner sense it more tangibly. Don't be afraid to experiment. Have your partner try to identify the energy shape being drawn upon them. Pay attention to what they describe and experience.

Compare it to what you discovered through the earlier exercise. What are the similarities and differences? What can you do to make the feelings more intense and identifiable? Switch places and allow your partner to draw patterns on you. Compare the similarities and differences.

Gradually increase your distance from your partner. How far can you stand away and still experience the energy pattern? Does it feel different when you extend the distance? Pay attention to the responses, which increases your overall sensitivity to subtle energies and their effects upon you.

Through these exercises you begin to train yourself to recognize those feelings that let you know when something is impacting upon your energy field.

18

Auric Field & Psychic Protection

Increasing numbers of people around the world are ready to gather in groups of understanding and love, which are generally referred to as "New Age" groups, or "light workers," but there are others as well. People are more open to receive information from higher levels of guidance, like the teachers of the Hierarchy. These groups can call on the Hierarchy with power if they so choose. There is a great responsibility to do this work with truth and integrity.

If you choose to be a part of this work to help humanity, please consider what your own soul is telling you to do, and furthermore, you should find the right group to be affiliated with, all within the Divine Plan.

Understanding Your Inner Voice

You should be aware of the information coming to you from within your own subconscious in order to realize when you are in rapport with the other people around you. When the messages are coming from your own soul, your life becomes in tune and organized to be of more service to the Divine Plan for Earth.

The Christ and His teachers are available to be called upon for help and direction, after which your life becomes more guided. With time and practice, you learn to distinguish where these ideas are coming from. It is wise to determine if ideas are coming from your guides and teachers, or somewhere else. As you learn to discern the source of these messages, a more direct communication becomes possible, and the more familiar you are with receiving message, the easier it is to produce accurate thoughts, ideas, and concepts to help humankind. Once you

Auric Field & Psychic Protection

receive these ideas and thoughts, you can put them into practical application through teaching, writing, and presentations, which is a normal and natural unfoldment of spiritual development, which helps others.

As we work with these thoughts and ideas, we open ourselves up to receive more information into our fields of consciousness. Our auric field then becomes a magnetic center of light and knowledge to be distributed to others who can be helped with this information. The key is our auric field, which affects our associates, and it is not necessarily our words that produce reactions, even though they are supposed to, it is really the vibrations of our auric fields.

Many things can be determined when a clairvoyant person, who can see colors, and energy, reads an auric field. Many times, if the person is sick, the auric field can be affected. It is a good idea to cleanse the auric field daily through different techniques that can be easily found. It is important that you find a technique that resonates with you. I personally use Archangel Michael for this type of work. He is very available to be called upon at any time to help with clearing out negative energies.

The energy around a person has an attraction; it can hold a group together, or keep an audience listening. It can make a person magnetic to gather others of like vibration. A person who is working through the heart and higher chakras can inspire hundreds. These chakras are brought into activity by love, wisdom and understanding — not by meditation or concentration upon the chakras.

Master teachers are so developed through their chakras that they swing one chakra into the other becoming a center of living light. Their chakras look like they overlap, making them look like they are surrounded with brilliant white light that can be hard to look upon with the naked eye.

Being Aware of the Dark Forces

We must be continually aware of our auric fields and be vigilant about clearing ourselves and using psychic defense, especially when we are light workers on the path of initiation and ascension. When we get to a certain level on the path with the ascended masters, we can become a target for dark forces, who are also present in the world. It is very important that light workers become aware of some of the methods that are used by the dark forces to lure unsuspecting persons in the wrong direction. The dangers can come into your auric field if you use drugs or alcohol, lose consciousness, or engage in careless sex, because these are some of the ways discarnate spirits can enter your body.

Always remember that it is important before starting your day, and before you sleep at night, to call on the Light to surround and protect you throughout the day, and while you are sleeping. It is best to use Archangel Michael to help

Possession

One of the dangers from discarnate spirits is that of possession, which can be of a temporary nature lasting for a few moments, or it can sometimes be for a longer period of time. It can even be a permanent situation lasting for the lifetime of the person. When you try too hard to receive information, the dark forces can pretend to be your guide or teacher. We must first of all call in the Light to protect us before we open ourselves up to other levels. It is good to call in Archangel Michael at this point to surround yourself in Light and protection before you open yourself up to call on your guides or teachers. I will go into some techniques for you to use for protection later on in this chapter.

When you are at the mercy of a possessing entity, you can be used against others, or for whatever the dark forces might need you. You become an unconscious and unwilling partner in this transaction.

Another cause of possession can be when the auric field of a person has a hole in it. Usually such a person is physically weak, or feeble-minded, but possessed with a powerful emotional body that suffers and fights to prevent entrance. These attacks are intermittent and more frequent on women than men.

Another cause can be emotional problems that occur when you are completely driven by your emotions without any restraint from your higher spiritual levels. This is the most common form of possession, and it affects those with powerful physical bodies. It can lead to struggles, such as screaming lunatics, or the seizures of the epileptic. Men are more subject to this than women, as women are usually more in touch with their emotional bodies.

A rarer type of possession is on the mental level, which involves displacement, which lets the possessing entity take control of person's physical and emotional body. It can be caused when the person has a strongly overdeveloped mind and a relative weakness in the emotional and physical bodies. This rare possession can attack women and men equally and usually shows up in childhood, which makes it harder to cure.

A very serious type of possession that is definitely the work of the dark forces is the snapping of one's magnetic cord, leaving the person in their emotional and mental body, which would normally result in the death of the physical body. However, in cases such as these, the dark possessing brother enters the physical body and makes a connection with his/her own cord. These cases usually involve highly evolved persons on the path, who, through some willful shortcoming, fail during a life. This great soul suddenly plunges on an apparent downward path, changing the whole trend of his or her life-changing the person from a good person to one who is overcome by the dark side. On the inner planes, the person looks on, and, in agony of mind, sees their actions dishonor their formerly good name, causing evil to be said of them.

Some of the other ways a discarnate spirit can find another body to possess is when suicides are anxious to undo the deed and to again get into contact with Earth. In addition, there are earthbound spirits, good and bad, who, from anxiety over loved ones or incomplete business affairs, eagerness to do wrong or to undo some evil act, rush in and take possession. Occasionally visitors from other planets can enter certain highly evolved bodies for purposes of their own; these are referred as "walk-ins."

Treatments

Different treatments can be used to heal the soul who is trapped by a possessing entity. One method is by hypnotherapy by one who is trained in this field to remove these entities. Violet light can be played over the body or certain sounds can be used.

If a person is being attacked at night, a mantra can be used to call the real owner back, and build a wall to keep the would-be possessor out. Hypnotherapy can also be used to call the possessing entity out of the invaded body. Additionally, shamans around the world use their own methods for doing soul retrieval.

Often, when a person is ready to be used by the Great White Brotherhood in service for the Light to help others, the dark brotherhood will begin its work to keep this from happening. These dark forces are alerted when the person's vibration have risen to a high-enough level to be of real use to the White Brotherhood, and the dark forces feel that it encroaches on their domain, at which time the person might be attacked on the mental, physical, emotional, or spirit level. They might be attack the physical body by disease, or by crippling it. Not all accidents happen by chance — some can be orchestrated by the dark forces.

Another method the dark forces use is to cast a cloud of emotional or mental distraction over a person, hiding what is real and true. This smoke screen is usually cast on the emotional level, making it hard to determine the real from the unreal. A typical example would be to cast a strong thought of weakness, discouragement, or criticism over a person, hoping that the person might give into these ideas. The unsuspecting persons don't realize that they are only seeing outlines of their own momentary thoughts, but instead they give way to discouragement, even to despair. When this happens, they are of little use to the ascended masters.

Another method a possessing entity can use is to throw suggestions and ideas into the person's mind, pretending they come from the person's own guide or teacher, but which are really subtle suggestions that hinder, rather than help. You must always use discrimination between the voice of your real teachers, and the false whispers of the evil ones.

There are many subtle ways used to deceive, and thereby curtail the effective output of light workers in service. We must be aware of our energy field, and call in the light of protection. When we protect our auric field and use discernment, we cut down on the risks of being led astray.

This information is given as a warning and guidance — not to cause alarm. Being aware of the many ways in which we can be led astray by the dark forces is a good thing. When we familiarize ourselves with their techniques, we can better understand what is happening to avoid and stop these activities. There are certain laws that limit and govern the activities of the dark forces.

The dark brothers are misguided and wrong in their ways — but they are still people, sparks of God, who have gotten on the wrong path. God has not given up on them, and they do have the opportunity to change. Many people get on the wrong path, but they can change over a period of time with perseverance and love. When a person does not listen in spite of warnings and pain, they eventually become a companion of darkness.

The dark forces do not respect any person; they only see people to be used or exploited for the furtherance of their own ends; they are self-centered. They use everyone they can to get their own way. By fair means or foul, they seek to break down all opposition to get what they desire. They don't care what suffering they might cause or what agony of mind they bring upon anyone. They persist in their intention, and don't refrain from hurting any man, woman, or child, provided that their own ends are furthered. Expect absolutely no mercy from those opposing the Brotherhood of Light.

It can appear that the dark forces have more power than the Brothers of the Light on the physical and emotional levels, but the Brothers of Light could exert their authority on these levels, but they choose to refrain instead, working with the powers of evolution to bring about change instead.

The dark ones can use elemental forces — like the elementals on the Earth, the gnomes, some of the brownies, and fairy folk who are colored brown, grey, or other dark colors — to cause many problems for people. The dark forces do not control the fairies who are colored blue, green and yellow, though a few of the red fairies can be made to work under their direction. Dark forces use some of the lower water elementals to do their bidding, but not the dolphins, whales, sea lions, or otters.

Sometimes the dark brothers pretend to be agents of the Light; often they pose as a messenger of God, but for your assurance, if you act under the guidance of your higher self, you will have clear vision and will escape deception.

At this time the dark brothers use these deceptions on the people with lower vibrations, because so few people have built the higher vibrations that attract the Brothers of Light, who move entirely on the two higher levels. When people reach these higher levels of vibrations, the attacks of elementals or lower level entities may be felt, but effect no harm, so the necessity of pure living and controlled pure emotions and elevated thoughts are a must.

The dark brotherhood is not dominant on the mental levels as they are on the physical and emotional levels. The mental level is the plane on which the Brotherhood of Light works. Mighty dark magicians are located on the lower mental levels, however, this is the plane where the White Brotherhood dominates. The three higher levels are where the ascended masters beg the evolving human beings to see and become aware — it is their region, to which all must strive and aspire. The dark

Auric Field & Psychic Protection

brothers retard progress and strive to shape all to their own ends. The Brothers of Light bend every effort to speed up our evolution. The Brotherhood of Light is foregoing all that might be theirs as the price of achievement, and they stay amid the fog, strife, evil, and the hatred of this time period. By staying on Earth, the members of the Brotherhood seek to help us all toward the Path of Light.

Methods for Protection

To safeguard against the dark forces in the world, purify your mental, emotional, and physical bodies so the dark forces cannot enter. When the dark forces enter our bodies, they must have been invited in by us in some way, which is why we need to purify our thoughts, words, and deeds. We must watch ourselves and keep our thoughts, words, and deeds positive at all times, not allowing anything on the negative level to enter.

First and foremost, call in the Light to protect yourself before opening up to other levels. It is good to call in Archangel Michael at this point to surround you in light and protection, especially before calling in your guide or teacher, so the other energies and influences cannot slip in. Archangel Michael is standing ready to help all light workers to keep these dark forces at bay while we are working with the Light.

We must guard against negative emotions like fear, hate, lust, anger, lying, jealousy, etc. We must eliminate all fear, for the forces of Light vibrate more rapidly than those of the dark, and within this fact lays a recognizable security, because fear causes weakness, which causes disintegration. A weak spot breaks open, and a gap appears in our auric field, and through that gap evil forces may enter. The factor of entrance is the fear of the person who opens the door.

Another thing we must do is to stand firm and unmoved, no matter what occurs. Your feet may be in the mud of earth, but your head will be bathed in the sunshine of the higher regions. [Recognition of the filth of earth involves no contamination. What?]

Use common sense in all situations, and get lots of sleep. While you sleep, learn how to keep your body protected and positive. Keep busy on the emotional levels and keep an inner calm. Refrain from overtiring your body, and play whenever possible. Relaxation helps us handle the times of tension.

God is within, no matter what happens on the outside, so when we call on the Light of God to protect ourselves, stay focused and centered at all times; we cannot be reached or hurt on our inner level.

19

Intuition & Mental Telepathy

Light workers are expanding their abilities in intuition and mental telepathy. In order to be more effective in these areas, it is important to train your mind to understand the subtle impressions that you receive from higher levels. These impressions are given by the teachers to the students to help them make the right decisions and choices that will affect their spiritual paths.

There are groups forming all over the world, so that no matter where you travel, you may come across some of these loose-knit groups in every neighborhood, and more groups will form in the coming years. These like-minded people are coming together to work on higher levels of energy healing like Reiki and reconnection. Usually massage and other body work are done, along with various forms of sound and color work to cleanse the auric field and remove blockages in the group members' etheric energy fields.

Hypnotherapy helps people deal with their fears, phobias, and health problems, and it may also address many soul issues from this and past lives. When we clear out all the issues we no longer need, we can move forward much more easily in a more healthy way. Many different techniques are used for energy work in the groups; there are no set rules as to how the work is to be done.

These groups will have increasing responsibility placed on their shoulders by the teachers, who will nurture the growth of telepathic interplay in the group, and the world. These strands of intuition and telepathic growth will eventually bridge the present gap between the seen and the unseen. This is so people realize that there is more to be seen and addressed than we can sense with our eyes alone.

Intuition & Mental Telepathy

We often see television shows and books about near-death experiences. People who contact spirits on the other side help us to understand that there is much more to be experienced after death than oblivion. Death is not the end of consciousness on a soul level; we are learning more about what happens to a soul after death. The soul continues on in another realm, and they know what is happening on the Earth to their families and loved ones. The deceased spirits send messages to their families through mediums who can tune into other energy levels, which leads to many wonderful experiences for people who used to think that death was final. It is important for people to contact their loved ones, so they can have closure.

Many people are opening up to learning more about the other side and things they may not understand. Their state of awareness is open and questioning, which helps them better understand how it all works. We begin to realize that everything is made of energy vibrating at different frequencies, thus creating many different dimensions. Nothing is static; the energy is vibrating, moving, and changing colors as the different vibrations are registered.

The auric field changes color according to the emotions we feel each moment. Auras are part of our etheric body, which is not seen with the naked eye. Now, scientists are finding that all living creatures have these auras.

The electromagnetic field affects all humans, but it cannot be seen or sensed in any way on a conscious level. The electromagnetic field is all around us, affecting our mental, physical, and spiritual levels. There are many ways in which the electromagnetic field affects us without our conscious knowledge. Very small magnetic fields influence our pineal gland. Several research groups have shown that applying a magnetic field of half a gauss or less in a certain way can cause an increase or decrease of production of melatonin and serotonin in the pineal gland. Low-frequency electromagnetic fields can cause confusion, short-term memory loss, stress, disease, and many other problems without our conscious knowledge. These fields are all around us today, but the extremely low frequency (ELF) transmissions have a peculiar property: because of their interaction with the ionosphere, even weak signals in this frequency range (from 0.1 to 100 cycles per second) travel all the way around the world without dying out.

Dowsing involves an unconscious sense of the electromagnetic fields of underground water or minerals. These techniques were given some support by Russian experiments in the 1960s, whose research showed the accuracy of 40 professional dowsers diminished by at least 3/4 when they wound a current-carrying wire around their wrists or brought a horseshoe magnet near their heads.

Some of the electromagnetic frequencies being used today are microwave, radio wave, X-ray, cell phones and the Wi-Fi technology. The ever-present hum of electromagnetic information may become an intolerable burden for humans and other creatures. Think how confused you would feel if you could simultaneously hear what everyone else in the world was thinking. After all, mediums and psi experimenters all agree that some sort of trance or mental quietude — a reduction of nerve impulse activity — is needed for best results.

The yogis of some Tibetan traditions teach clairvoyance to novices by having them meditate seated on a glass plate, facing north toward a sheet of polished copper in a dark, windowless room. There is a bar magnet suspended over their heads, its north pole pointing up to the zenith.

It is generally known that American power lines are based on 60-Hz electric fields, which have been linked to bone tumors in mice, slowed heartbeat in fish, and various chemical changes in the brain, blood, and liver of rats. Russian researchers found that bees exposed to a strong ELF field for a few days began to sting each other to death or leave the area. Others sealed off their hives and asphyxiated themselves. Additional tests were done regarding increasing the electrical field frequencies around rats. The results showed the rats to have severely stunted growth, stressful reactions, and greater weight gain than normal. It also revealed large increases in the infant mortality rate of newborn rats.

This evidence to date suggests that electro-pollution is presenting us, and perhaps all animals, with a double challenge with weaker immune systems and stronger diseases. When human cancer cells were exposed to 60-Hz electromagnetic fields for just 24 hours, a six-fold increase in their growth rate was found seven to 10 days later.

In the early 1960s it was found that when microwaves of 300 to 3,000 MHz were pulsed at specific rates, humans, even deaf people, could "hear" them. The beam caused a booming, hissing, clicking, or buzzing, depending on the exact frequency and pulse rate. The sound seemed to come from just behind the listener's head. Later work showed that the microwaves are sensed somewhere in the temporal region just above and slightly in front of the ears. The phenomenon apparently results from pressure waves set up in brain tissue, some of which activate the sound receptors of the inner ear via bone conduction, while others directly stimulate nerve cells in the auditory pathways.

We should pay attention to this information, because many people today are experiencing sounds of different kinds in their ears. It is commonly being treated by the doctors as tinnitus, but it could be caused by all the electro-pollution.

In addition to certain frequencies negatively affecting people, there are several ways of controlling their behavior. Research in this area has shown that microwaves modulated in various ways can force specific electrical patterns upon parts of the brain. Working with cats, researchers found that brain waves appearing with conditioned responses could be selectively enhanced by shaping the microwaves with a rhythmic variation in amplitude (intensity) corresponding to EEG frequencies. For example, a 3-Hz modulation decreased 10-Hz alpha waves in one part of the animal's brain, and reinforced 14-Hz beta waves in another location.

These are some examples of how we can be affected on other levels without our knowledge. The electromagnetic fields of the Earth are caused in part by the planet's molten iron core, and the charged gas of the ionosphere, and they change at different times of the month, as we orbit around the sun. The field of the Earth is about 10 Hz. Solar flares are also sending charged particles to Earth, and every flash of lightning releases a burst of these electromagnetic energies. Large direct currents also continually flow within the ionosphere as telluric (within-the-Earth) currents, generating their own subsidiary electromagnetic fields. The potential interactions between all these different electromagnetic fields of the Earth are very complex.

Everything in the world is governed by vibrations or frequencies, and humans are no exception. Frequencies can be used to heal, regenerate, and help humankind, or they can be used for destructive purposes. It would be better for all of us if we could ensure that they are only used for constructive purposes in the world.

We cannot do much about the sun or Earth's fields, but we can reduce the 60-Hz devices in our homes by decreasing or eliminating the use of microwaves and Wi-Fi devices, or, at the very least, turn them off at night.

20

Group Activities for Service

Certain things must be in place before the Christ can walk among the people of this world once again. People's vibrations must reach a certain level, with the preparatory work already done. Light workers and others are helping to prepare the world for the return of the Christ. Spiritual teachings through the ages have been concerned with gathering knowledge, and do not give back enough for what is received. The masters instruct us to produce good works, not only acquiring knowledge and working for individual attainment, but also taking actions helping free all humankind and the Earth.

Only during the 20th century has such a balance been given. This balancing was done through the knowledge and activity of the students invoking the powers of the Light. They were taught invocation by issuing decrees, particularly in unison, because there is more power in unified action, each having the combined effort of all. By singing devotional songs, the groups also produce much energy that can be used by the Light.

When we as a group focus our thought in a unified direction it creates an outgoing stream of energy. This stream will telepathically reach those who are sensitive to receive it. This thought energy will act to create on the physical level what is being called into manifestation. I have been doing some of this type of work with groups of people who know their thoughts are powerful. Focusing a group's thoughts like a laser creates change. When we are working with this energy, it is very important to always be aware of our positive intent.

As we move further into intuition and telepathy, more of this work will be done by people who realize how important it is to project a

Group Activities for Service

stream of energy with focused intent. All creations in the universe are manifested from the spoken word, written word, or thought energy. The amount of energy released in songs, decrees, visualization and contemplation in group activity is amplified by the number participating. It is a good way to quickly balance our account back to life.

Through decrees we can contribute energy from the physical realm, which is taken up and used for the specific purpose to be handled. Great service is being rendered by amplification in group activity — we have the combined power of the group. The same principle applies in pushing a car or lifting a weight. If two people each push on his or her own car, it may not move; but when both push on the same car at the same time, they have enough power to get results. Besides that, in group work, the effort of each individual is amplified by the number of the group, which is as if each individual gave the decree as many times as there are persons in the group.

Through group activity much assistance is given to the locality. Much of the daily mass accumulation and destructively qualified energy can be transmuted and released, which helps keep the atmosphere pure.

By using "I AM" statements in groups, the co-operative action of people working from the same principle blesses all the group, because the I AM Presence is in each one of us.

One-third of the energy must be released from humans in our physical realm of self-conscious effort; two-thirds of the energy will be supplied by the masters. Sixty percent of the energy released in decrees and songs for devotional purposes stays in your own world, and 40% goes into service.

The Aquarian Age is bringing in new energy to facilitate the seventh Ray — the Ray of freedom. It will be the predominant vibration for the Earth for the next 2300-year cycle. It activates the energy of purification and redemption. The Violet Flame — the flame of transmutation — is the divine alchemy which resurrects and perfects energy. It provides us the opportunity to make things right. The ceremonial Ray enables the individual to consciously change the quality of energy at will, in themselves and the world about them. It also gives us the opportunity to render cosmic service along with individual development.

The transmutation of energy is a conscious action that results in divine alchemy, which is a science — a drawing of energy into a form or condition to change it. This transmutation is done through unified words of calling it or visualizing it as a group while focusing the energy. When the intelligence in that energy acts, substance changes. Individuals are ordinarily unconsciously changing the pure energy they receive from the I AM Presence with imperfect qualities. This new transmutation energy activity is to change and qualify energy consciously into perfection again by transmuting it.

The Violet Flame was brought to Earth by St. Germain through Godfrey Ray King in the "I AM" books. This flame is a great opportunity for humanity because it can be used to return the substance of anything that has fulfilled its service and is of no further use back to the universal level.

Energy continues to go on until it is transmuted. The Violet Flame is used in all the higher realms. It is used by divine and ascended beings to etherealize whatever has come forth in any realm that was not used as well as it should have been, or has completed its service. The energy can be returned back to that particular realm for use again, once it is transmuted.

The transmuting Violet Flame can be used for purification, but it is also used to invoke or magnetize, and radiate. This is its use on other planets, where it is not required for purification as it is on Earth. The idea is to draw the Sacred Fire through the power of invocation, which is done through the power of thought, feeling, and the spoken word.

It is known that rapid vibrations rise; they are drawn to the realms of light where the frequency is higher, while the slower or heavier ones descend or sink, and stay in Earth's atmosphere, which is why the

Group Activities for Service

perfection from the realms of light must be drawn down to Earth. In order to do this, there must be a magnetic center by which it is drawn and then radiated out. This center can be created consciously by individuals and groups.

People must use the power of invocation by calling to it with conscious intent to use it in this realm where it is to be put into action. This invocation will bring the energy to the situation that needs to be changed. Applying this process in a group of people who are consciously and collectively decreeing impersonally while willing the good of the whole will create greater results that are magnified according to the size of the group.

This new energy of the Aquarian Age is to teach humankind how to draw, qualify, and radiate it outward, creating Life, in a new manner that will increase the glory of the planet and all evolution on it. An action of the seventh Ray in the new age is to bring in energy that supports a brotherhood among humans, as well as the conscious and tangible association between angels, men, women, children, and the elementals. It is expressed through ordered service, and it becomes a ritual of daily life. It is the action of rhythmic invocation and radiation. Rhythm comes under this Ray — the returning to one's activity of service rhythmically - near the same time daily.

The activities and qualities of the seventh Ray of the Aquarian Age are rhythmic application, transmutation, invocation, magnetization, radiation, and ordered service, diplomacy, courtesy, refinement and culture. The color is violet and purple, and the jewel is amethyst.

In the future when we no longer live as separate societies with different beliefs, all the people of the world will observe the same holy days every year.

The Festival of Easter is the Festival of the risen, living Christ, the Teacher of all men and the Head of the Spiritual Hierarchy. He is the Expression of the love of God. On this day the spiritual Hierarchy, which He guides and directs, will be recognized and the nature of God's love will be emphasized. This Festival is determined always by the date of the first Full Moon after the spring equinox on March 21st.

The Festival of Wesak is the Festival of the Buddha, the spiritual Intermediary between the highest spiritual center, Shamballa, and the Hierarchy. The Buddha is the expression of the wisdom of God, the embodiment of Light and the Indicator of the divine purpose. This will be fixed annually in relation to the next full moon after the Festival of Easter.

The Festival of Goodwill is the Festival of the spirit of humanity aspiring towards God, seeking conformity with the will of God and dedicated to the expression of right human relations. This will be fixed annually in relation to the next full moon following the Wesak Festival. It will be a day when the spiritual and divine nature of mankind will be recognized. On this Festival for two thousand years the Christ has represented humanity and has stood before the Hierarchy and in the sight of Shamballa as the leader of His people and "the Eldest in a great family of brothers." (Romans VIII:29). Each year at that time He has preached the last sermon of the Buddha, before the assembled Hierarchy. This is a festival of deep invocation and appeal, of a basic aspiration towards fellowship, of human and spiritual unity, and it will represent the effect in the human consciousness of the work of the Buddha and the Christ.

The time is coming when all three Festivals will be kept throughout the world and by their means a great spiritual unity will be achieved and the effects will be stabilized by the united invocation of humanity throughout the planet.

The other full moons throughout the year will be recognized as being very important. They will establish the divine attributes in the consciousness of people, just as the major holy days help to establish the three divine aspects. These will be studied to understand what energies are coming from the particular constellations that are influencing these months.

21

The Law of Light

Ancient civilizations of the world were talking about the "Light," which is one of the laws of the universe. The ascended masters teach that "the Light" shall flood the Earth and its people, and whatever cannot stand the radiance of that Light must disappear, like mist before the morning Sun.

The law of life of the whole universe is the "law of light," and before its blazing glory and invincible power, all discord and chaos are consumed.

Everywhere about us is a universal substance we call "Cosmic Light," which the Bible refers to as Spirit, which is the one pure primal essence out of which all of creation comes. It is the pure-life substance of God. The Light is infinite, and we may draw upon it any time we need to. Pure Light is the great limitless storehouse of the universe. In it is all perfection, and out of it comes all that is.

The law of Light does not receive inharmonious energy into itself. As we enter more into this Light, we become perfection. The disharmony will drop away from our body and affairs when we let go of all thought, feeling, and words about imperfection. An activity that will always bring complete freedom to you is to show unconditional love and eternal forgiveness to everybody and everything.

The law of life is to give, for only by giving of yourself can you expand. To give the intense love of your own God self to all humankind and to all life is the greatest activity you can use to draw divinity into yourself. In this way, Divine Love is made up of every good thing.

When you sincerely forgive, you will find your world reordered as if by magic, and filled with every good thing. However, remember that unless discord is forgotten, it is not forgiven, because you cannot lose it or release yourself from it until it is out of your consciousness. Therefore, as long as you remember an injustice or a disturbed feeling, you have not forgiven either the person or the condition.

When the forgiveness is complete, the emotional body is serene, kind, happy, and comfortable and becomes a mountain of Light. It is so powerful that one resides within it as in a fortress. Even though you stand among the wreck of worlds, you will remain untouched by anything but perfection of the Light.

Remember, that which your consciousness is held firmly upon, you bring into existence in yourself. It is impossible for your life to contain anything that is not your present or past accumulation of consciousness. Whatever you are conscious of in thought and feeling stamps itself upon the energy in and around you bringing forth more energy of its kind. This is a cosmic law from which there is no variation or escape.

Divine Light is the reservoir of life and the treasure chest of the universe. It automatically draws to you every good thing. When the outer activity acknowledges this divine Light in everything and every way, then all things are accomplished without struggle or strain. Life never struggles, for that which struggles is the consciousness that attempts to limit life, and it is but the interference with the perfection that is forever trying to come through. If the personal or outer self will just "let" life flow and remain at peace, the manifested result will be perfection — the divine way of life fulfilled.

All we need to do to bring something we desire into form is to hold the conscious attention upon the visualized form. This creates a focus for the concentration and brings the energy to us for this thought we are manifesting. Our feeling, united with the mental picture, sets up a magnetic pull. The law of like attracts like is the universal law that people utilize during their lives. When working with this law, there must be a certain amount of knowledge of how to raise your vibratory rate.

As we study this particular condition of Light, and how we are to use it, we must maintain a certain state of consciousness in order to attain the goal. It must be done with a definite positive knowing feeling. We must not allow doubt or fear to enter, and we must keep a positive attitude.

Divine love is the heart of infinity and of the individual. It is an ever-flowing, intelligent flame that releases energy, wisdom, power, and substance without limit. It will release boundless blessings to all who will harmonize their own personalities enough to let it come through.

This pure divine light can always be called upon to dispel darkness, for the divine Light of God never fails.

22

Opportunities for The Future

Humanity should be looking for massive changes that Mother Earth is preparing to gift us. These changes are occurring because we have outstripped resources all over the world, with a huge population that has threatened our very existence by not holding the Earth sacred. We have not respected the Earth and her bounty. Our modern societies have only taken from the Earth, with no thought of tomorrow, or how the resources we have squandered, misused, and wasted will be replaced. The Earth gives and She can take away. The energy of the Earth works in a reciprocal fashion, and when we do not operate in this fashion, She will retaliate to protect Herself.

We must prepare for the coming times, because we have brought them upon ourselves. We should learn to become more self-sufficient in order to survive in the days ahead. It will be beneficial to know how to grow our own food, how to live off the land, and how to give Mother Earth the respect She deserves. We can show respect for Her by using some of the techniques of the Native Americans, and by doing ritual and ceremony to show our appreciation for the bounty She has given us.

Mother Earth has given us so much that we assume that it is a never-ending process. We should learn to protect our clean water, and make sure it is taken care of for the future of humankind.

The people of the Earth are facing some tough decisions, if they do not change, because Mother Earth will take measures to protect Herself. These changes will come in the form of catastrophes such as extreme weather, earthquakes, volcanoes, and huge displacements of water. The time for change is now! Change cannot be put off by the people who think they have ways of getting around global consequences, or assume they will be untouched. Nothing can conquer Mother Earth, especially when it comes to people who are arrogant, selfish, greedy, and uncaring of others who are less fortunate. No matter how much money these people may have, it will not save them from the wrath of Mother Earth.

The Native Americans were very advanced, because they realized the importance of respecting the Earth, and making sure that they left nothing behind to pollute it in any way. We certainly could have learned from them. They knew we are all One, and that whatever you do to others, you do to yourself. They hold the circle sacred, for the energy always comes back to the one who first sends it out — this is the law of the universe. Our words, thoughts, and deeds come back to us through others in our lives. The Earth will send back to us what we have given Her. Taking this into account presents a whole new picture of the situation.

Our fossil fuel reserves are dwindling, and industry is taking a terrible toll on Mother Earth by fracking and otherwise ripping resources from the earth. For our benefit and survival, we must develop alternative energies and get them on the market. They must be allowed to reach the public. The inventions already have been given to humankind, but the ones in control have bought the patents, or resorted to worse methods to control these new technologies from being used by the people of the world.

Many people of the world have been praying for change. The spiritual teachers have heard the call, which has reached the higher spiritual levels, and God has responded to this call. Christ has been sent back to us to correct evil things that are happening today. It is time for humankind to have an opportunity to come back to the Light. We have been sent a glorious group of teachers who have come to help humankind get on the right path back to God. The Christ Spirit and His disciples have returned to bring all people of the Earth into the Divine Light of God.

The Great White Brotherhood and Christ and His disciples, who are here on Earth to help as great teachers sent by God, stand by to help humanity make the right choices. It is time for us to learn more about these great teachers and what they have to offer us. The true shift coming will be on an inner level of consciousness, which is in the process of gradually happening now. Once we shift from the negative-ego mind set to spiritual Christ Consciousness, on a mass scale, how we act and think will be changed — we will be centered in our souls instead of our negative ego.

Sirius is where the Great White Lodge of the Solar Hierarchy is found. From it come those who act as Messengers of the Wisdom of God, custodians of the truth as it is in Christ, and those whose task it is to save the world, to impart the next revelation, and to demonstrate divinity. Sirius has been helping and guiding mankind for millions of years.

Christ spoke of those who have come from the spiritual center to which Christ gave the name "the Kingdom of God" (Matt. VI:33) in order to reveal the love of God. Here dwell the "spirits of just men made perfect." (Heb. XII:23); here the spiritual Guides of the race are to be found and here the spiritual Executives of God's plan live and work and oversee human and planetary affairs. This place is located on Sirius and has been called by many different names down throughout time. Today it is known as the Great White Lodge of Sirius, and this Solar Hierarchy works with the Planetary Hierarchy called the Great White Brotherhood and Shamballa where the Planetary Logos, Sanat Kumara resides.

The spiritual Hierarchy has been steadily drawing nearer to humanity as people have become more conscious of divinity and more advanced in their understanding in order to approach the divine. This will help bring about a universal brotherhood of fellowship and world cooperation and peace, based on right human relations.

When the people of the world come together at the same time the power of their united invocative thought of the masses will create an outgoing stream of energy. This will telepathically reach those spiritual Beings who are responsive and sensitive to such impacts. Their evoked response, sent out as spiritual energy, will in turn reach humanity making an impact upon the minds of people, convincing them and carrying on inspiration and revelation.

In the future the ego and the spirit will work in harmony, much like the specific parts of a cell, working together in perfect union. We don't normally analyze the specific parts of a cell to see if they are working properly. When we reach harmony, our ego and spirit will function together as a whole. Each of us is a cell in the body of God. When ego and spirit are integrated, each of us will be a healthy cell in God's body.

Our challenge is to become focused on our connection to God and to be of service as we have never been before. Each person is a part of God, and no one will be overlooked. It is time to see people as equals, regardless of their state of spiritual development, their social standing, or where they are from in the world, or what race they might be, for we are all the same in the eyes of God. Each person is a specific incarnation of God, with a purpose, a mission, and an attribute of God's infinite nature that only they can express in a certain way.

It is time for the light workers to move into a new phase of service, because most of them will be called upon to teach others who have not been attuned to their spiritual path. The ascended masters of the Great White Brotherhood have been communicating through light workers and others on a huge scale since the Harmonic Convergence in 1987. The light workers have rallied together and created a whole new way of life. The time for light workers who have been riding the fence has come to an end; now it is time to use what we have learned to be of service to others. We must all come to a new level of understanding to raise people's vibrations. As we help our brothers and sisters move along the path of understanding, we are helping ourselves, and all of humanity.

We light workers must stand as good examples by projecting harmlessness toward others. When we come from a place of harmlessness, we bring about a caution in judgment of others, reticence in speech, the ability to refrain from impulsive action, and the demonstration of a non-critical spirit, which gives free passage to the forces of true love of others, and to those spiritual energies that seem to vitalize our personality, leading us to right action.

When we let harmlessness be the keynote of our life, other good things will blossom forth from it. When we practice harmlessness of thought, in our emotional reactions, and in our acts, we are allowing ourselves to be open to attract higher vibrations of a positive nature that will bring us closer to God.

As light workers, we must learn to work with energy at all times in our life. To be conscious of the energy around us, and to transmute it when needed. We are here to learn to control, transmute, and send energy for the good of others. To manage and control energy and substance is mastery. The nature of energy is action, and destructive force is qualified energy expressing that quality. Pain is qualified energy, and it takes energy to produce pain and to feel it. We can command it to change. Call to the Christ Presence to re-qualify the energy with ease, peace, and perfection. We must realize we have the power to call on the divinity within that connects us to the Christ Consciousness.

Energy can be used for constructive or destructive purposes. It is like the rain that falls to the Earth, because it falls on good and evil alike. Therefore, energy must be directed into constructive channels and be used for the good of all. We as light workers, must become aware of this fact and begin to use it constructively to help the world.

This is a wonderful time to be alive. We all have the opportunity to step into our Christ Consciousness with the help of the Christ, His disciples, and the ascended masters who have come to assist humanity to find their way back to the Light. It is a great blessing to be incarnated at this time in Earth's history, for there has never been anything like it in terms of opportunities for spiritual growth.

Opportunities for The Future

With the ending of this cycle on December 21, 2012, we received a new opportunity to become One with the Light and with the alignment of certain stars and constellations. We were given the opportunity to begin a new way of life that will take us on the road to recovery. Many have been aware of these changes.

Revelations 21 talks about a "New Heaven and a New Earth," which I believe is bringing us an opportunity to start a new cycle called the Aquarian Age, which, if used correctly by humankind, can turn this world around toward God once again. We must use this opportunity to change our ways — to begin treating Mother Earth and ourselves with respect, love, and realization that we are all One.

23

Spiritual Hierarchies

The Solar Hierarchy

The Solar Logos

The Solar Trinity

First Department:

    The Father includes Will or Power

Second Department:

    The Son includes Love-Wisdom

    1. The Seven Rays
    2. Three Rays of Aspect
    3. Four Rays of Attribute

Third Department:

    The Holy Spirit-Active Intelligence includes:

    4. Harmony and Beauty
    5. Concrete Knowledge
    6. Devotion and Idealism
    7. Ceremonial Magic

The Emerging Planetary Hierarchy

Sanat Kumara: The Lord of the World
    AKA The Ancient of Days
    AKA The One Initiator
The Three Kumaras
    Assistants, Buddhas of Activity
First Department - Will:
    The Manu
    Master El Morya
    Master Jupiter
Second Department - Love-Wisdom:
    The Bodhisattva - The Christ-World Teacher
    Master Kuthumi
    Master Djwal Khul
    Four grades of initiates, grades of disciples
    People on the Probationary Path
    Average Humanity of all degrees
Third Department - Active Intelligence:
    Master Serapis Bey
    Master Hilarion
    Master Jesus
    Master St. Germain

24

Bibliography

CHAPTER 1 THE AQUARIAN AGE
A Vision of the Aquarian Age, George Trevelyan, Stillpoint Pub., Walpole, NH.

CHAPTER 2 MOVING TOWARD CHRIST CONSCIOUSNESS
King James Bible: St. Luke (C9:28-29)
King James Bible: St. Mark (C12:30-31)
Edgar Cayce Companion, Ernest Frejer, Barnes & Noble, Inc.
Ancient Mystical White Brotherhood, Rev. George Graham Price, Great Seal Press.
King James Bible: St. John (C2:17)
Life And Teaching Of The Masters Of The Far East, Vol. 3, Baird T. Spalding, DeVorss Publications, Camarillo, CA.

CHAPTER 3 UNIVERSAL ONENESS OF RELIGION
The Complete Ascension Manual, Joshua David Stone, Light Technology Pub., Sedona, AZ.
Lives Of The Master, Glenn Sanderfur, A.R.E. Press, Virginia Beach, VA.

CHAPTER 4 COMING EVOLUTIONARY CHANGES
The Secret Doctrine Vol. II, H.P. Blavatsky, Theosophical Pub. House, Wheaton, IL.
The Masters And The Path, C.W. Leadbeater, Theosophical Pub. House, Wheaton, IL.

CHAPTER 5 SIRIUS AND COSMIC EVOLUTION

Bibliography

Reappearance Of The Christ, Alice A. Bailey, Lucis Pub. Co., New York, NY.
The Lost Star, Walter Cruttenden, St. Lynn's Press, Pittsburgh, PA.
The Secret Doctrine, H.P. Blavatsky, Theosophical Pub. House, Wheaton, IL.
Sirius, Maureen Temple Richmond, Source Pub., Mariposa, CA.
King James Bible: St. Matthew 6:33; Hebrews 12:23, Job 38:31.

Chapter 6 Solar Hierarchy of Sirius
Sirius, Richmond (Ibid.)
Cosmic Ascension: Your Cosmic Map Home, Joshua David Stone, Light Technology Pub., Sedona, AZ

Chapter 7 Space is Cosmic Consciousness
Cosmic Ascension, Stone (Ibid.)

Chapter 8 Sanat Kumara-Planetary Logos
Law Of Life And Teachings, A.D.K. Luk, Vol. 2.
The Secret Doctrine, Blavatsky, (Ibid.)
The Reappearance Of The Christ, Bailey (Ibid.)
The Masters And The Path, Leadbeater (Ibid.)
The Complete Ascension Manual, Joshua David Stone, Ph.D. Light Technology Pub., Sedona, AZ.

Chapter 9 Shamballa-Home Of Sanat Kumara
The Masters And The Path, Leadbeater, (Ibid.)
Law Of Life And Teachings, Vol. 2, Luk (Ibid.)

Chapter 10 Departments Of The Hierarchy
The Complete Ascension Manual, Stone (Ibid.)

Chapter 11-Who Are The Masters Of Wisdom
Ancient Mystical White Brotherhood, Price (Ibid.)
Law Of Life And Teachings, Luk (Ibid.)
The Masters And The Path, Leadbeater, (Ibid.)

The Complete Ascension Manual, Stone (Ibid.)
Masters Of The Far East, Baird T. Spalding, Vol. 4, DeVorss Publications, Camarillo, CA.

CHAPTER 13 ST. GERMAIN--MAHA CHOHAN--LORD OF CIVILIZATION
The Masters And The Path, Leadbeater, (Ibid.)
Law Of Life And Teachings, Luk (Ibid.)
The Complete Ascension Manual, Stone (Ibid.)
The Seventh Ray, Alice A. Bailey, Lucis Trust, New York, NY.

CHAPTER 14-WHAT IS ASCENSION?
The Complete Ascension Manual, Stone (Ibid.)
The Rays and The Initiations, Alice A. Bailey, Lucis Trust, New York, NY.
Ancient Mystical White Brotherhood, Price (Ibid.)

CHAPTER 15 PURIFYING YOURSELF FOR ASCENSION
The Complete Ascension Manual, Stone (Ibid.)
Hypnosis For Change, Josie Hadley & Carol Standacher, New Harbiner, Canada.

CHAPTER 16 REGENERATION OF THE BODY
The Healer's Manual, Ted Andrews, Dragonhawk Pub., Jackson, TN.
Life Forces: Guidelines For A Healthy Life On A Polluted Planet, Jill Collings; New English Library, Kent 1991.

CHAPTER 17 ETHERIC BODY & CHAKRA SYSTEM
The Book of Chakra Healing, Liz Simpson, Gaia Books, London.
The Healer's Manual, Andrews (Ibid.).

CHAPTER 18 AURIC FIELD & PSYCHIC PROTECTION
Infinite Mind, Science Of The Human Vibrations Of Consciousness, Dr. Valerie Hunt; Malibu Pub. Co., CA.
Understanding Auras, Joseph Ostrom, Thorsons, London, 1987

BIBLIOGRAPHY

Psychic Protection, Ted Andrews, Dragonhawk Pub., Jackson, TN.

CHAPTER 19 INTUITION & MENTAL TELEPATHY
Telepathy, Alice A. Bailey, Lucis Trust Pub., New York, NY.

CHAPTER 20 GROUP ACTIVITIES FOR SERVICE
The "I AM" Discourses, Godfre Ray King, St. Germain Press, Inc., Schaumburg, IL.

CHAPTER 21 THE LAW OF LIGHT
Law Of Life And Teachings, Luk (Ibid.)

CHAPTER 22 OPPORTUNITIES FOR THE FUTURE
Bible: Rev. Chapter 21.

INDEX

A
Abraham 25
ADD (attention-deficit disorder) 34
ADHD (attention-deficit-hyperactivity
      disorder) 34
adrenal glands 35
Age of Enlightenment, 51
Alcyone, Central Sun 48
Ancient of Days, see Sanat Kumara
angels 74
animals 5, 75
apsi (same position in relation to the
      starting point of the cycle) 36
Aquarian Age 1, 2, 3, 5, 7, 8, 13, 14, 39,
      47, 50, 74, 75, 110, 112, 113, 174,
      176
Archangel Gabriel 26, 28
   as teacher of Mary and Joseph (St.
      Germain) 28
Archangel Michael xi
Archangel Zadkiel' 117
Arcturians 53
   Why Earth is now beginning to work so
      closely with them 53
Arcturus 152
Aryasanga 79
AS (Asperger's syndrome) 34
Asaph, the Prophet 25
ascended masters 28, 73–100
   do not eat food 74
Ascended Masters of the Great White
      Brotherhood, see also
      Hierarchy 7
ascension 19, 121–128
   defined 121
ASD (autistic-spectrum disorder) 34
Asia 63
Association of Research and Enlightenment
      (A.R.E.) viii
Atlantis 8, 24, 37, 41, 46, 76, 110
   as Atlantic prolongation of Lemuria 37
   sinking of 98
auric field 157, 159, 168
avatar, defined 103
awareness of energy 154

B
Babylon 26, 48
Bailey, Alice 93, 127
balance 120, 173
Beauty 189
Bhagavad-Gita 27

Bible 21
Blavatsky, H.P. 31, 48, 61, 90, 92
blending East and West 8
Board of Elders ix
Bodhisattva 26, 190
Brothers of Light 163
Buddha 13, 75, 77–79, 81, 177
   brought Light 13
   Portrait 78
   teacher of the East 13
Buddhism 27
   Tibetan 28

C
chakras 60, 146, 148
changes in sexual practices 118
chela, defined 92
Cherokees 48
children
   medicated 34
   television 34
Christ 43, 46, 76, 80, 100, 157, 173, 185
   as Jesus, 18
   as Maitreya 27
   brought Love 13
   in us 17
   many incarnations of 24
   meaning of the second coming 82
   teacher of the West 13
Christ Consciousness 2, 3, 6, 11, 12, 14,
      15, 19, 21, 56, 123
   as the consciousness of the soul rather
      than the ego 82
Christ Spirit 112
   as Hindu Master Krishna 79
   as Lord Maitreya 79
   as Tsong-ka-pa 79
   incarnations 11
Christianity 27
church of Christ 16
churches 86
Cody, Darla
   1998 visit with Sai Baba 105
   as student of Djwhal Khul 92, 93
compulsion to talk 122
Confucianism 28
consciousness raising 12
coronal mass ejections (CMEs) 32
cortisol 35
cosmic triangle 47
Council of Nicaea 24
Cowan. Walter, resurrection 106

195

INDEX

crucifixion 126
Cruttenden, Walter 42

D
Daniel 59
dark forces 49, 158
  still sparks of God 162
Department
  First 189, 190
  Second 189, 190
  Third 189, 190
depression 138
Devotion 189
displacement 160
distraction 161
Divine Plan 16, 41, 113, 157
Djwhal Khul 28, 37, 42, 44, 46, 47, 48, 68, 69, 90–93, 95, 98, 127, 128, 190
  as a wise man 28
  as Aryasanga 92
  as Confucius 28, 92
  as first chela of Buddha 92
  as Gai Benjamin 90
  as Kleinias, Pythagoras's favorite pupil 92
  as teacher of Darla Cody 92, 93
  helping to put this book together 93
  known as "The Tibetan" 90
  known as Master D.K.," 90
  materializing 92
  on Lemuria 92
  portrait 91
DNA 42
Dogons 42
  knew of Sirius B before astronomers 42

E
Earth changes 35, 117, 183
  preparation for 183
Easter 176
Edgar Cayce viii, 24
Egypt 25, 39, 42, 44, 98
El Morya 32, 68, 71, 87–90, 92, 95, 113, 190
  as a Rajput prince in India 90
  as Abraham 28
  as future Manu, or Ruler, of the sixth root race 88
  as King Arthur 90
  as Melchior, a wise man 89
  as poet Thomas Moore 90
  portrait 88

  working with three groups of angels 89
electromagnetic energy 43
electromagnetic field 168
electromagnetic frequencies 169
elementals 163
emotions 164
empathy 34
Essenes 25, 27
ether 49
  element of the Fifth Sun, celestial and lacking in material substance 49
etheric body 145
Eve 24, 110
evolution 31, 84
exercises 156

F
fatigue 138
Feminine energy 109
Festival of Goodwill 177
Fifth World 39, 41, 65
fight-or-flight response 35
Flame of Truth 95
Focus of Truth 95
forgiveness 180
Freemasons 113, 114
frequencies 171

G
Galactic Logos
  defined 53
Garden of Eden 110
Genesis 24, 25
glands 146
Gobi Desert 40, 63
Gobi Sea 63
God 43
  breath of 55
  Fatherhood of 73
  in all kingdoms of Nature 17
  self-surrender to 20
governments to fall 6
Great Bear 9, 47, 53, 54
  expresses will or purpose 47
  includes Arcturus 48
Great Central Sun 40, 44, 47, 51
Great Flood 52
Great Pyramid 39
Great White Brotherhood ix, xi, 27, 39, 40, 44, 46, 64, 111, 117, 124, 127, 161, 185
  Himalayan branch 63

196

INDEX

Great White Lodge 41, 44, 46, 47, 185
group activity 174

H
Hall of Learning 131
Hall of Wisdom 131
Harmonic Convergence 4
Harmony 189
Hebrews 46, 185
Helios 53, 54
Hercules, El Morya's teacher 90
Hermes, see Enoch 25
Hierarchy 7, 18, 19, 28, 40, 41, 44, 46, 61, 62, 73, 75, 77, 84, 88, 100, 115, 124, 125, 128, 145, 157, 177, 185
  Department of the World Mother 108–110
  Departments of the 67–71
  Emerging, chart of 190
  First Department or Ray 68
  Office of the Christ 82
  Planetary 190
  Second Department or Ray 68
  six masters of the
    Djwhal Khul 77
    El Morya 77
    Hilarion 77
    Kuthumi 77
    Paul 77
    St. Germain 77
  six masters of the Hierarchy 77
  Solar 189
  Third Department or Ray 69
    five sections 70
Hilarion 93–96, 113, 190
  as a priest in the Temple of Truth on Atlantis 95
  as Chohan of the Fifth Ray 96
  as John the Beloved, a disciple of Jesus 95
  as Lamblichus, of the Neoplatonic School 95
  portrait 94
Himalaya 92
Himalayas ix
Hinduism 27
Holy Roman Empire, 24
Holy Spirit-Active Intelligence 189
hormones 137
Human avatars
  Abraham Lincoln 43

  Buddha 43
  Jesus 43
  Plato 43
hypnosis 135
hypnotherapy 167

I
I AM Presence 174
Idealism 189
India ix
initiates 190
  fifth-degree 64
  no boasting 14
initiation 17
  as love expressing itself through wisdom 15
  fifth 49, 127
  first 123
  fourth 82, 126
  second 123
  second, also Baptism 18
  sixth 82
  third 18, 32, 56, 124
intelligence 144
intuition 31
Isis 39
Islam 27
  birthed by Jesus as Muhammed's guide 26
  founding of 79

J
Jacob 25
James 11
Jerusalem 26
  meaning 83
Jesus 11, 12, 20, 21, 75, 77, 98–100, 113, 126, 153, 190
  as a Syrian in the 1600s 100
  as Adam 24
  as Amilius in Atlantis 24
  as Apollonius
    travels 100
  as Apollonius of Tyana 99
  as Asaph 25
  as Enoch 24
  as Jeshua 26
  as Joseph 25
  as Joshua 25
  as Melchizedek, taught Abraham how to start Judaism 25
  as Muhammad's spiritual teacher 26

INDEX

as Zend, father of Persian avatar
    Zoraster 26
ascension 12
at the Temple of the Jews 15
five major examples in His life 12
overlighted by Christ Consciousness 11
portrait 99
resurrection 12
trained by the Essenes 25
why He is called the Christ 27
Job 46
John 11, 23, 24
John the Baptist 18
Jordan River 12, 82
Judaism 27
    started by Jesus as Melchizedek 25
Jupiter 68, 190

K

King David 25
King Solomon 25
King, Godfrey Ray 116, 175
Kingdom of God 11, 15, 31
Knowledge 189
Krishna 13, 75, 79–84, 104
    portrait 80
Kumaras 190
Kumaras, defined 60
Kundalini 150, 153
Kuthumi 32, 69, 85–87, 90, 92, 95, 113, 128, 190
    and Theosophy 87
    as Balthazar, a wise man 87
    as Pythagoras 29, 86
    as Saint Francis of Assisi 87
    as St. Francis of Assisi 29
    Bodhisattva of the sixth root race 85
    current incarnation 86
    portrait 85
    to become Chohan of the Second Ray 85

L

Lao Tse 28
Law of Attraction 54
Law of Cause and Effect 16
law of Light 179
Law of Rebirth 16
Leadbeater, C.W. 40
Lemuria 37
    cradle of the third root race 37
    location 37
light workers 1, 14, 157, 167, 186

time to come together 49
Logos
    Cosmic 55
    Planetary 32, 54, 55, 56
    Solar, see Solar Logos 54
Lord Maitreya 27, 67, 68, 69
    as Lord Krishna 27
    head of the Spiritual Hierarchy and the Great White Brotherhood 26
    overlighting Jesus 27
love 66, 181
Love-Wisdom 189
Luke 11
Luxor 98

M

Madagascar 37
Madhavacharya 79
Magic 189
magnetic cord 160
Maha Chohan 60, 67, 69, 70, 90
Mahabharata 27, 104
Mahachohan 69
Maitreya 77, 79–84, 90
    "overlighted" Jesus 82
    as Kuthumi's teacher 86
    current incarnation 82, 83
    portrait 81
    the Planetary Christ 82
Man, Brotherhood of 73
Manu 68, 69, 71, 88, 190
    Allah Gobi 67
Mark 15
masculine energy 110
master portraits
    Serapis Bey 97
Masters Of Wisdom 73–100
masters' portraits
    Buddha 78
    Djwhal Khul 91
    El Morya 88
    Hilarion 94
    Jesus 99
    Krishna 80
    Kuthumi 85
    Maitreya 81
    Paul 101
Matthew 46, 185
Mayan calendar 39, 41
Mayans 44, 63
Melchior, Galactic Logos 53
Melchizedek 25, 75

mercy 163
microwaves 170
Middle Way 77
Milky Way 43, 53
monad, defined 124
moon 36
Moses ix, 25
Mother Mary, see World Mother
Mount Carmel 11, 12, 18, 24
Mount Golgotha 12
music 130

N
Nagarjuna 79
Native Americans 141, 183, 184
near-death experiences 168
New Age 1, 109, 117, 157
Nile River 39, 98
Noah 52
Nommo, amphibious gods from Sirius 42
Norway 37

O
ODD (oppositional-defiance disorder) 34
oneness 141, 188
Order of Franciscan Friars 87
Order of Melchizedek 25, 27
Order of St. Clara 87
organic food 129
Orpheus 100
overlighting, defined 82
oxygen 140

P
paradigm shift 118
Patanjali 139
Pathway of Power 54
Paul
  portrait 101
PDD (pervasive developmental disorder, somewhat like autism) 34
Peter 11, 24
Pharaoh 25
Piscean Age 12, 74
pituitary gland 35
Planetary Hierarchy 190
 , see Great White Brotherhood
Planetary Logos 68
Pleiades 9, 46, 47, 48, 54, 152
  Arabs had two names for them 48
  express active intelligence 47
  Temennu — the Foundation Stone. 48

pole shift 31
possession 159
Power 189
Prana 139, 149
precession of the equinox 41, 43, 50
Prema Sai Baba 105
Probation 190
proof 21
protection methods 164
Prozac 34
Psalms 26
psychic protection 157
purification 129, 175
Pythagoras 99, 100

R
Rachel 25
Ramanujacharya 79
Ray 60
  defined 55
  Fifth 94, 96
  First 88
  Fourth 96, 98
  Second 55, 69, 90, 93
  Seventh 96, 98, 117
  seventh 112, 174
  Sixth 100
  third 112
Rays
  Aspect 189
  Attribute 189
  seven 189
Reiki 153
reincarnation 23
  excised at Council of Nicaea 24
rejuvenation 137
renunciation 126
resurrection 127
Revelations 188
Ritalin 34
Romans 177
root race
  Aryan 31
  Atlanteans of the fourth 37
  climate change in sixth 35
  fifth 31, 113
  Master Kuthumi, Bodhisattva of the sixth 32
  Northern Lemurian third 37
  seventh will be last 31
  sixth 56, 68
    starts in California 32

Round, Fifth 61
   "judgment day" 62

S

Sai Baba x, 103–110
   as Shirdi Sai Baba 104
   coming foretold over 5,000 years ago 104
   incarnation of Vishnu 104
   materializations 106
   Oneness 107
   portrait 103
   raising the dead 106
   Virbutti ash 107
Sanat Kumara 18, 32, 40, 44, 54, 56, 57, 59–62, 64, 67, 123, 124, 145, 190
   also the Lord of the World, the One Initiator, the Ancient of Days, Melchizedek 60
   areas of power 60
   Council Chamber of 65
   portrait 59
   see also Logos, Planetary
Sathya means truth in Hindi 104
self-will 20
sensitivity 154
Serapis Bey 70, 96–98, 113, 190
   and the Colossus at Rhodes 98
   and the League of Nations 98
   and the Parthenon 98
   and the Seraphim 98
   and the temples of Thebes and Karnak 98
   as a priest in the Ascension Temple on Atlantis 98
   as Chohan of the Fourth Ray 98
   as King Leonidas of Sparta 98
   as Phidias in Athens 98
   as the Chohan of the Fourth Ray 96
   current incarnation 96
shaman
   no boasting 14
Shamballa 18, 32, 60, 62, 63–66, 113, 123, 177
   the City of White 63
Shankaracharya 92
SID (sensory-integration dysfunction) 34
Siddhartha Gautama, see Buddha
sidereal year of 25,868 solar years 36
sin, saved from 47
Sirians helping humankind 39
Sirius 9, 28, 47, 54, 56, 152, 185

A 45
B 45
C discovered 45
cosmic energy from 40, 43, 45, 48
distance from Earth 39
expresses love-wisdom 47
Great White Lodge of 40
home of Great White Brotherhood 26
sleep 165
Solar Hierarchy 189
Solar Logos 54, 152, 189
   defined 53
   three departments — The Father, The Son, and Active Intelligence 53
Solar Trinity 189
Sons of Asaph 26
South Africa 37
South America 63
Space
   as a cosmic being 57
   as a field 57
spiritual purpose 50
Spiritual Triad 19
Sri Yukteswar 51, 52
   as teacher of Paramahansa Yogananda 50
St. Germain ix, 67, 69, 70, 71, 95, 96, 111–120, 175, 190
   and sound 119
   as "the Count" 113
   as a priest in the Temples of Purification and the Violet Flame on Atlantis. 117
   as Andreas 114
   as Cervantes 114
   as Christopher Marlowe 114
   as Columbus, the explorer 114
   as Comte de Gabalis 114
   as Director of the Transmuting Violet Flame 117
   as Edmund Spencer 114
   as Francis Bacon 114
   as Francis Tudor, heir to the throne of England 114
   as Godfrey Ray King 28
   as Hungarian Prince Rakoczy 114
   as Joseph 28
   as Joseph, the husband of Mother Mary 114
   as Lord of Civilization 111
   as Maha Chohan 112
   as Merlin in King Arthur's court 114

as Montaigne 114
as Robert Burton 114
as the father of modern democracy in America 115
as the inspiration and power behind the Magna Carta 116
as the Jewish prophet Samuel 28, 114
as the power behind Napoleon 116
as the son of Queen Elizabeth I 114
as translator of the King James Bible. 115
portrait 111
startle flickers 34
sub-root race
  characteristics of children in sixth 31
  fifth 113
  intelligence of the fifth 32
  lasts 20,000 years 31
  physical, mental, and spiritual characteristics of the sixth 33
Sumeria 44
sunshine 130

T

Taj Mahal 87
Taoism 28
telepathy 31
television 168
Temple of the Ascension Flame 98
Temple of Truth 96
Tertiaries Order 87
Theosophy 89, 92, 116
third-eye center 125
thyroid 137
Tibet 92, 169
time speeding up 75, 129
time to blend the ancient teachings of the East and the West 76
transfiguration 18, 24
treatments 161
Tristan Da Cunha 37

U

Universal Oneness of Religion 23

V

Varuna, great guardian angel Lord 86
Vedic teachings 50
Venus 60, 63
  City of the Kumaras 63
Viavasvata Manu 35
vibrations 171

Violet Flame 174, 175
Vishnu 104
  as Sai Baba 104
visitors from other planets 160
vitamins 137
Vyassa
  as Gautama Buddha 27

W

Wesak 77, 177
What You Can Do 133
will 189
wisdom 32
Woodrow Wilson 97
working with the ascended masters of the 26
world cataclysm 62
World Mother 108
  as Deva 109
  as Kwan-Yin 109
  at Fatima 110
  chosen to birth Jesus 108
World Teacher 26

Y

yoga 139
Yuga 50
  Dwapara 50
  Kali 50, 104
  Satya (Golden Age) 51
  Treta (Silver Age) 51

Z

Zend 26
zodiac 46
Zoroastrianism
  influenced by Jesus as Zend 26

Printed in Great Britain
by Amazon